PEARSON LONGMAN

CORNERSTONE

4

PEARSON English Learning System

Workbook

Anna Uhl Chamot

Jim Cummins

Sharroky Hollie

PEARSON

Upper Saddle River, New Jersey • Boston, Massachusetts • Chandler, Arizona • Glenview, Illinois

Pearson Longman Cornerstone 4
Workbook

PEARSON English Learning System

Staff credits: The people who made up the Cornerstone team, representing editorial, production, design, manufacturing, and marketing, are John Ade, Rhea Banker, Daniel Comstock, David Dickey, Gina DiLillo, Johnnie Farmer, Nancy Flaggman, Charles Green, Karen Kawaguchi, Ed Lamprich, Niki Lee, Jaime Lieber, Chris Leonowicz, Tara Maceyak, Linda Moser, Laurie Neaman, Leslie Patterson, Sherri Pemberton, Diane Pinkley, Liza Pleva, Susan Saslow, Chris Siley, Loretta Steeves, Kim Steiner, and Lauren Weidenman.
Text composition: The Quarasan Group, Inc.

ISBN-13: 978-1-4284-3487-
ISBN-10: 1-4284-3487-

Printed in the United States of America
8 9 10 V0N4 16 1

CONTENTS

CONTENTS

Name _____ Date _____

Key Words

Use with Student Book pages 8–9.

| young |
| protect |
| secure |
| communicates |

A. Choose the word that *best* completes each sentence. Write the word.

1. Most animals _____ their babies from danger.

2. Baby wallabies feel warm and _____ in their mother's pouch.

3. Adult animals teach their _____ how to care for themselves.

4. A mother _____ with her babies by making sounds.

B. Choose the word that *best* matches the meaning of the underlined words. Write the word.

5. Shells <u>give a safe place to</u> turtles and snails. _____

6. Birds feed worms to their <u>small babies</u>. _____

7. Baby animals feel <u>safe</u> when their mothers are near.

_____

8. A bird <u>sends a message to</u> other birds when it sings.

_____

3

Academic Words

Use with Student Book page 10.

challenge
goal
involve

A. Match each word with its definition. Write the letter of the correct answer.

1. involve _____   **A** something hard to do

2. goal _____   **B** include, or be part of

3. challenge _____   **C** something you want to achieve

B. Choose the word that best completes each sentence. Write the word.

4. Her most important _____ in life was to be an astronaut.

5. He accepted his friend's _____ to ride his bike up the steep hill.

6. My mother told me to _____ my little brother in the game I was playing.

C. Answer the questions.

7. Have you ever said no to a **challenge**? Why?

_____

_____

8. What **goals** did you have last year?

_____

_____

 **Write a paragraph telling what you know about animals and their young. Share your paragraph with a family member.**

Name _____ Date _____

Phonics: Short Vowels

Use with Student Book page 11.

> A word is likely to have a short vowel sound when:
> - it has a single vowel.
> - the vowel has a single consonant before and after it (CVC)

Circle the words with the CVC pattern. Then write the short vowel sound. The first word is done for you.

1. (pin) _short i_____

2. sad _____

3. hot _____

4. food _____

5. wet _____

6. cube _____

7. him _____

8. sky _____

9. bag _____

10. red _____

 Brainstorm a list of ten words with the CVC pattern. Share your words with a family member.

Comprehension: Taking Care of the Young

Use with Student Book pages 12–19.

Answer the questions about the reading.

Recall

1. Why is it hard for baby swans to escape danger on their own?

   _____

2. Where do mother raccoons leave their babies when they look for food?

   _____

3. What is a baby wallaby called?

   _____

Comprehend

4. How do both male and female emperor penguins take care of their babies?

   _____

   _____

Analyze

5. How are human parents and animal parents similar?

   _____

   _____

   _____

Name _____   Date _____

Reader's Companion

Use with Student Book pages 12–19.

Taking Care of the Young

Raccoon babies are very small when they are born. They cannot stand or open their eyes. Only female raccoons take care of the babies. A mother might have four babies to take care of alone. She must leave them in the den when she looks for food. In the den, the raccoon babies are safe from danger.

The mother raccoon worries that other animals might find her den. So after a few months, the family moves. By then, the babies can walk and climb. Their mother has taught them to take care of themselves.

Use What You Know

List three things you know about raccoons.

1. _____
2. _____
3. _____

Reading Strategy

What are raccoons like when they are born? Underline one sentence that tells you.

Comprehension Check

Circle the sentences that explain which parent takes care of the raccoon babies.

Use the Strategy

Why does the mother raccoon move her family? Reread the passage to find the answer.

_____

_____

_____

Retell It!

Retell this passage as if you are a zookeeper. Tell a group of children about raccoons.

_____

_____

_____

_____

_____

Reader's Response

Which of the animals would you like to learn more about? Why?

_____

_____

_____

Copyright © by Pearson Education, Inc.

Retell the passage to a family member.

Name _____　Date _____

Learning Strategies: Reread for Details

Use with Student Book pages 22–23.

Read the passage below. Reread to help answer the questions.

Unusual Horses

Seahorses are unusual animals. You might think a seahorse is a horse that likes to swim. Seahorses do swim! But they don't have legs. They can't even live on land. Seahorses are fish.

Seahorses look different from other fish. A seahorse's head looks a bit like a horse's head. Many seahorses also have tiny fins. And seahorses have a tail that can curl up under them. Seahorses use their tail to hold onto plants, and sometimes each other.

One unusual thing about seahorses is their pouch. Other animals have pouches, too. But among seahorses, the father has the pouch. He keeps the eggs safe until the babies are ready to be born.

1. How do you think the seahorse got its name?

_____

2. What can a seahorse do with its tail?

_____

3. How is a father seahorse different from a mother seahorse?

_____

Share what you learned about seahorses with a family member.

9

Grammar: Simple Present

Use with Student Book pages 24–25.

Review the different forms of the **simple present tense**.

I/You/They/We	walk	don't walk	to school.
He/She/It	walks	doesn't walk	to school.

The verb *be*

I	am	am not/'m not	
He/She/It	is	is not/isn't	hungry.
You/They/We	are	are not/aren't	

Complete each sentence with the correct simple present tense form of the verb.

Example: (run) I <u>run</u> when the weather is bad.

1. (protect) The mother _____ her young until they can climb to safety.

2. (eat) We _____ everything on our plates.

3. (not travel) I _____ in an airplane to see my cousins.

Circle the correct form of the verb *be* that *best* completes the sentence.

Example: We **is /** (**are**) hungry after basketball practice.

4. I **are / am** tired after school.

5. **Is / Are** you happy with your grades?

6. He **is not / aren't** excited to see the movie.

Write five sentences about your favorite animal. Use three **simple present tense** verbs and two forms of the **be** verb to describe how it acts. Share your sentences with a family member.

Name _____ Date _____

Spelling: CVC Pattern

Use with Student Book pages 26–27.

SPELLING TIP

Notice that the word *him* has the CVC pattern.

A. Fill in the blank with a vowel to make a word with the CVC pattern. Some examples have more than one choice.

1. h _____ t

2. c _____ p

3. p _____ n

4. r _____ g

B. Fill in the blank with a consonant to make a word with the CVC pattern. Some examples have more than one choice.

5. no _____

6. ca _____

7. _____ it

8. _____ an

 Write two sentences. Use a CVC word in each sentence.

_____

_____

Home-School Connection Use the examples above to write three additional CVC words with the short vowel sound. Share your words with a family member.

Writing: Describe an Animal

Read the paragraph. Then read each question and circle the correct answer.

(1) I am at the children's zoo with my class. (2) The zookeeper shows us an African gray parrot the bird is beautiful. (3) It has a powerful curved beak. (4) On each foot it has four toes with long claws. (5) It's feathers are smooth and gray. (6) There is a white band around the bird's eyes. (6) It's eyes look intelligent. (7) The parrot's bright red tail feathers gleam in the sunlight. (8) This amazing bird learns many words and other sounds. (9) When our class leaves, the parrot calls, Good-bye!"

1. What change, if any, should be made in sentence 2?
   A Change *shows* to *showed*.
   B Change *parrot the bird* to *parrot. The bird*
   C Change *an African gray* to *a African gray*
   D Make no change

2. What is the BEST way to revise sentence 4?
   A The bird has two feet with long claws.
   B Each of the four toes has long claws.
   C One each foot are four toes with really long, scary claws.
   D No revision is needed.

3. What change, if any, should be made in sentence 5?
   A Change *smooth and gray* to *smooth gray*
   B Change *are* to *were*
   C Change *It's* to *Its*
   D Make no change

4. What change, if any, should be made in sentence 9?
   A Change *Good-bye!"* to *"Good-bye!"*
   B Change *Good-bye!"* to *"Good-bye?"*
   C Change *calls* to *answers*
   D Make no change

Name _____ Date _____

Key Words
Use with Student Book pages 28–29.

| shimmer |
| frisky |
| glowed |
| warm |
| breath |
| companion |

A. Choose the word that *best* completes each sentence. Write the word.

1. He saw a star _____ in the sky.

2. The campfire kept us _____ during the cold night.

3. A small light _____ in the darkness.

4. The _____ animals jumped and rolled through the tall grass.

5. I ran until I was out of _____ .

6. A pet can be a person's best _____ .

B. Choose the word that *best* matches the meaning of the underlined words. Write the word.

7. The moon <u>gave off a soft light</u>. _____

8. I felt <u>a little hot</u> under the heavy blanket. _____

9. My pet is my favorite <u>friend and playmate</u>. _____

10. Divers hold their <u>air in their lungs</u>. _____

11. At night, lights <u>shine softly</u> on the water. _____

12. Puppies are <u>lively and playful</u>. _____

Academic Words

Use with Student Book page 30.

| bond |
| encounter |
| occur |

A. Choose the word that *best* completes each sentence. Write the word.

1. My grandfather and I have a strong _____ because we both love to go hiking.

2. We gave our dog a bath after her _____ with a skunk.

3. School may be canceled tomorrow, if snow _____.

B. Choose the word that *best* matches the meaning of the underlined word. Write the word.

4. We shared a <u>special connection</u> because we both liked to play baseball. _____

5. Our birthdays <u>happen</u> on the same day. _____

6. When you <u>come to</u> a stop sign, look before crossing. _____

C. Write a sentence using each word.

7. What **bond** do you and a friend share?

_____

_____

8. Why does rain **occur**?

_____

_____

Use each key word in a sentence. Share your sentences with a family member.

14

Name _____   Date _____

Word Study: Endings -s, -es, -ed

Use with Student Book page 31.

> Add *-ed* to a word when you want to show something that happened in the past. Add *-s* or *-es* to a word when you want to show something that is happening now.

A. Put a check in the boxes that tell about each word when *-s,* *-es,* or *-ed* is added. The first one is done for you.

	-s happening now	*-es* happening now	*-ed* happened in the past
1. walked	☐	☐	☑
2. plants	☐	☐	☐
3. filled	☐	☐	☐
4. rushes	☐	☐	☐

5. Write a sentence to tell what a friend does every day. Use one word ending in *-s*.

_____

6. Write a sentence to tell what a friend did yesterday. Use one word ending in *-ed*.

_____

Home-School Connection Write two sentences to tell what you did on your last birthday. Use words with the *-ed* ending. Share your sentences with a family member.

15

Comprehension: The Star Llama

Use with Student Book pages 32–37.

Answer the questions about the reading.

Recall

1. What did the boy and the old llama do every day?

_____

2. Where did the boy bury the llama?

_____

3. What shape did the star take?

_____

4. What happened when the star llama jumped back into the sky?

_____

5. What did the boy do with the wool?

_____

Comprehend

6. Describe the encounter between the boy and the star llama.

_____

_____

Analyze

7. In what ways were the old llama and the star llama similar?

_____

_____

_____

Name _____ Date _____

Reader's Companion

Use with Student Book pages 32–37.

The Star Llama

The star llama drank for a very long time. Then she looked at the sad Inca boy and smiled. When she jumped back into the sky, bits of llama wool fell. The boy felt the silver wool. It was soft and warm.

As the sun began to rise, the boy gathered the llama wool. It glowed in his hands like starlight. He carried the wool to the city and sold it. With the money, he bought a house and two frisky young llamas. He never forgot the star llama. And he was never lonely again.

Genre MARK the TEXT

In fables, animals often behave like humans. Underline a sentence that describes the llama acting like a human.

Reading Strategy

List two things that are fantasy.

1. _____

2. _____

Comprehension Check

Draw a box around one sentence that is reality.

Use the Strategy

What happened when the llama jumped into the sky? Reread the passage to find the answer. Tell if the answer is fantasy or reality.

_____

_____

_____

Retell It!

Retell this passage as if you are a storyteller visiting a class of younger students.

_____

_____

_____

_____

Reader's Response

What did you learn about the boy from the passage?

_____

_____

_____

Retell the passage to a family member.

Name _____ Date _____

Learning Strategies: Fantasy and Reality

Use with Student Book pages 38–39.

Read each statement. Do you think it is possible? Write R for Reality and F for Fantasy.

1. A duck lays one thousand eggs in a day. _____

2. The dog used different sounds to communicate. _____

3. His cat ran as fast as the car. _____

4. Scientists discovered a fish living in a tree. _____

5. New kinds of animals come to Earth from outer space. _____

6. Her pet goldfish lived for three years. _____

7. The stars are home to many animals. _____

8. The seagull lost a feather. _____

Home-School Connection Tell a family member one event that could be reality and one event that would have to be fantasy.

Grammar: Simple Past: *be* Verbs

Use with Student Book pages 40–41.

The **past tense** of *be* must agree with the subject.

I/ He/She/It	was	wasn't/was not	
You/We/They	were	were not/weren't	excited.

Complete each sentence with the correct negative past tense of *be*.

Example: He <u>**wasn't**</u> in school today because he's sick.

1. They _____ in the cafeteria during lunch.

2. _____ your mom waiting for you at the bus stop?

3. The knight's encounter with the dragon _____ in the movie.

4. _____ we supposed to go bowling tonight?

Rewrite each sentence from the present tense to the past tense.

Example: She is ready to go to the park.

She was ready to go to the park.

5. We are happy with your grade on the test.

_____

6. Isn't she funny wearing that costume?

_____

7. The class is on a field trip today.

_____

Write five sentences about something you did last summer. Use the **past tense of *be*** to describe what you remember. Share your sentences with a family member.

Name _____ Date _____

Spelling: Endings -s, -es, -ed
Use with Student Book pages 42–43.

A. **Add -s or -es to write the correct present-tense form of each verb.**

1. ask _____

2. push _____

3. hand _____

4. clap _____

5. watch _____

> ### SPELLING TIP
>
> Many present-tense verbs have the ending -s. For verbs ending in x, s, ch, sh, and z, add -es. Many past-tense verbs have the ending -ed. Remember to add -s, -es, and -ed when you write.

B. **Use the correct past tense verb to complete each sentence.**

6. We ran when the bear _____. (growl)

7. My pet skunk _____ living in the garage. (like)

8. He _____ the dishes after dinner. (wash)

9. She _____ with her friend every day. (play)

10. The boys _____ into the pond. (jump)

Write about an experience you had with an animal. Use three words used as answers on this page.

_____

_____

_____

Home-School Connection Write sentences using both the present and past tenses for two of the words. Share your sentences with a family member.

21

Writing: Describe Yourself

Use with Student Book pages 42–43.

Read the paragraph. Then read each question and circle the correct answer.

(1) When I was seven years old, I was at the swimming pool almost every day. (2) I were soaking wet. (3) It was summertime, and I was at the pool. (4) My swimming trunks were red, and my towel was blue with yellow and green stripes. (5) My knees were grass-stained and my front teeth was missing. (6) I lost it when I fell off my bike. (7) I remember that I would be very happy that day. (8) To me, the pool was the best place in the world!

1. What change, if any, should be made in sentence 2?
   A Change *soaking* to *soaked*
   B Change *I* to *It*
   C Change *were* to *was*
   D Make no change

2. What change, if any, should be made to sentence 5?
   A Change *knees* to *knee*
   B Change *teeth* to *tooth*
   C Change *and* to *but*
   D Make no change

3. What change, if any, should be made in sentence 7?
   A Change *I remember* to *I do remember*
   B Change *would be* to *was*
   C Change *happy that* to *happy, that*
   D Make no change

4. Which sentences do NOT belong in this story?
   A Sentences 7 and 8
   B Sentences 5 and 6
   C Sentences 3 and 4
   D Sentences 1 and 2

Name _____   Date _____

Key Words

Use with Student Book pages 44–45.

mustangs
feral
captured
breeders
banned

A. Choose the word that *best* completes each sentence. Write the word.

1. My mother told me not to go near

_____ animals.

2. After her bad behavior, she was _____ from the computer lab for a week.

3. The police _____ the bank robber outside the bank.

4. Do you think wild _____ should be allowed to run free?

5. The _____ want to find good homes for all of the puppies.

B. Write TRUE or FALSE.

6. Feral animals make good pets.   _____

7. You must handle captured animals with care.   _____

8. You are banned from reading books in school.   _____

9. Breeders take care of animal babies.   _____

10. Mustangs are a type of horse.   _____

Academic Words

Use with Student Book page 46.

establish
recover
strategy

A. Choose the word that _best_ completes each sentence. Write the word.

1. Our coach's _____ for the game is to run until the other team is tired.

2. To _____ from an illness stay in bed and eat healthy food.

3. The judge asked many questions in order to _____ the truth.

B. Write the word that _best_ matches the meaning of the underlined words.

4. My mom said in order to <u>get well</u> I had to stay inside all weekend.

5. We will draw out a <u>design</u> to find the treasure before we start looking.

6. I will <u>start</u> a lemonade stand on my street corner.

C. Write a sentence using each word.

7. What would you need to **establish** a new supermarket?

_____

_____

8. What is your **strategy** for doing well in school?

_____

_____

 Write two new questions. Each question should contain at least two of the key words. Share your questions with a family member.

Name _____ Date _____

Phonics: Long Vowels with Silent e

Use with Student Book page 47.

> These words follow the CVCe pattern. The first vowel in each word has a long vowel sound. The second vowel—the letter *e*—is silent.
>
> | a_e | e_e | i_e | o_e | u_e |
> |------|------|------|------|------|
> | game | Pete | hide | tone | rule |

A. Unscramble the letters to write a CVCe word.

1. e s n o _____

2. c a e f _____

3. n t e u _____

4. i e r c _____

B. Choose one vowel that will complete both words in the row. Write the vowel.

CVC Words	CVCe Words
5. m _____ d	m _____ de
6. t _____ b	t _____ be
7. h _____ p	h _____ pe
8. h _____ d	h _____ de

Think of another pair of words that follow the CVC and CVCe pattern shown in the chart above. Share them with a family member.

Comprehension: Mustangs

Use with Student Book pages 48–51

Answer the questions about the reading.

Recall

1. When did the first horses come to the western United States?

_____

2. What is a feral animal?

_____

3. How did mustangs help Native Americans?

_____

Comprehend

4. Who was Wild Horse Annie?

_____

_____

Analyze

5. What do you think would have happened to the mustangs if the Wild Free-Roaming Horses and Burros Act had not been passed by Congress?

_____

_____

_____

Name _____ Date _____

Reader's Companion

Use with Student Book pages 48–51.

Mustangs

When Spanish explorers came to America, they brought horses. The first horses came to the western United States in the 1500s. As the explorers traveled through the Southwest, some horses escaped. They lived in herds in the wild. By the 1800s, about two million horses roamed the American West.

****

Some Native Americans captured and trained mustangs. Native Americans became skilled at riding horses. Hunting and traveling became easier on horseback. Horses helped Native Americans carry their possessions when they moved.

Reading Strategy

Look at the title. List two things this passage could be about.

1. _____

2. _____

Genre

Reading selections always have a title. List two other titles you could give this passage.

1. _____

2. _____

Comprehension Check

MARK the TEXT

Underline how many mustangs roamed the American West in the 1800s.

Use the Strategy

Preview the first paragraph of the passage. What do you think happened to all these wild horses?

_____

_____

_____

Retell It!

Retell the passage as if you were a Native American with a new mustang. Write a journal entry about your horse.

_____

_____

_____

_____

Reader's Response

Write about an animal that helps other people. Explain why that kind of animal is helpful.

_____

_____

_____

Copyright © by Pearson Education, Inc.

Retell the passage to a family member.

Name _____ Date _____

Learning Strategies: Preview

Use with Student Book pages 52–53.

Read the title and answer the first question. Then read the passage and answer the second question.

The Unusual House Guest

When Melinda came home, her bedroom was a mess. The window and closet door were open. Her clothes were everywhere. "Mom," said Melinda, "Tilly has been in my room." Tilly was Melinda's younger sister. Sometimes Tilly liked to wear her older sister's clothes. But it wasn't Tilly. Melinda picked up her clothes from the floor. Then she heard a sound. "Aaaah!" she screamed. "Mom, there's an animal in my closet!"

1. What did you learn about the story from the title?

_____

_____

_____

_____

2. What do you predict will happen next?

_____

_____

_____

_____

 **Tell a family member about how well you were able to predict what the story was about.**

Grammar: Simple Past: Regular Verbs

Use with Student Book pages 54–55.

To form the **simple past tense** of most **regular verbs** add -ed.

We **sail** in the lake.	➞	We **sailed** in the lake.

To change some other verbs to the simple past look at the endings.

Add -d to verbs ending in -e.	live ➞ **lived**
Change the y to i and add -ed to verbs ending in a consonant and -y.	cry ➞ **cried**
Add -ed to verbs ending in a vowel and -y.	play ➞ **played**
Double the consonant and add -ed for verbs with a stressed CVC ending.	control ➞ **controlled**

Complete each sentence with the correct simple past tense of the verb.

Example: (capture) We **captured** the other team's flag.

1. (cure) The doctor _____ his patient.

2. (invent) Thomas Edison _____ many useful things.

3. (carry) I _____ the groceries home for my mother.

4. (melt) The snow finally _____ in early spring.

5. (admit) We _____ to breaking the bed after jumping on it.

6. (spray) Who _____ you with the garden hose?

7. (study) I _____ very hard all weekend for the test today.

8. (plan) Who _____ this surprise party?

9. (roam) Many wild mustangs _____ the American West.

Change the following verbs to **past tense**: *trade, worry, copy, carry,* and then write sentences for each. Share your sentences with a family member.

Name _____ Date _____

Spelling: CVCe Pattern

Use with Student Book pages 56–57.

A. Fill in the blank with a vowel to make a CVCe word.

1. My mother likes to b ____ ke.

2. Yesterday she m ____ de us cookies.

3. I h ____ pe she cooks us something today.

4. It takes a lot of t ____ me to cook.

B. Read each clue. Fill in the blank to complete the CVCe word.

5. you do it with your hands   w ____ ve

6. you live in it   h ____ me

7. you play it   g ____ me

8. you stand in it   l ____ ne

Write about something you did this week at home or at school. Use three CVCe words.

_____

_____

_____

_____

31

SPELLING TIP

Notice that the word *home* has the CVCe pattern. Remember to use the CVCe pattern when you write.

Writing: Describe a Place You Visit

Read the paragraph. Then read each question and circle the correct answer.

(1) Last summer my family visited a beautiful Beach near our home. (2) When we got closer to the ocean, I recognized the sharp smell of the salt water. (3) As soon as we arrived, my sisters and I jumping from the car and raced along the shore. (4) Some of the other kids talked to us. (5) The beach sparkled in the bright sunlight. (6) Then we rushed into the cold ocean water. (7) While the roaring waves carried us back to shore. (8) To warm up we buried our feet under the wet, smooth sand. (9) What an amazing day!

1. What change, if any, should be made in sentence 1?
   A Change *visited* to *were visiting*
   B Change *summer* to *sumer*
   C Change *Beach* to *beach*
   D Make no change

2. What change, if any, should be made in sentence 3?
   A Change *jumping* to *jumped*
   B Change *raced* to *racing*
   C Change *from the car* to *out of the car*
   D Make no change

3. What is the BEST way to revise sentence 7?
   A While the roaring waves carried us back to shore.
   B Suddenly the roaring waves carried us back to shore.
   C When the roaring waves carried us back to shore.
   D No revision is needed.

4. Which sentence does NOT belong in this story?
   A Sentence 4
   B Sentence 5
   C Sentence 6
   D Sentence 7

Name _____ Date _____

Review

Use with Student Book pages 2–57.

A. Answer the questions after reading Unit 1. You can go back and reread to help find the answers.

1. Which of the following questions is NOT answered by the end of *Taking Care of the Young*? Circle the letter of the correct answer.

   A Do male emperor penguins take care of their babies?

   B Do adult swans keep animals away from their babies?

   C Where does the father raccoon find food for his babies?

   D Do older joeys sometimes leave their mother's pouch?

2. How does a clown fish protect its eggs?

_____

3. Read this sentence from the selection.

> Mother wallabies have an unusual way to protect their babies.

What does *protect* mean?

   A watch   **C** hurt

   B trouble   **D** keep safe

4. What did the boy in *The Star Llama* do with the wool that fell from the sky?

_____

_____

5. Read this sentence from "Mustangs." Then underline the past tense verbs.

> Some Native Americans captured and trained mustangs.

6. Write a sentence about how Native Americans used the mustangs.

_____

7. Which word does NOT have the CVCe pattern? Circle the letter of the correct answer.

A home   **B** cat   **C** make   **D** like

8. Read these sentences from the story.

> As the explorers traveled through the Southwest, some horses escaped. By the 1800s, about two million horses roamed the American West.

What does **roamed** mean?

A got away   **C** many
B walked freely   **D** looked around

B. Read these sentences from _The Star Llama_. **Then answer questions 9 and 10.**

> The boy cried for a very long time. But there was no one to comfort him. One star began to shimmer. Slowly, the star took the shape of the old llama. When she jumped back into the sky, bits of llama wool fell.

9. Circle one simple past form of _be_.

10. Find one sentence that tells the reader the story is a fantasy. Then find one sentence that tells about something that could happen in real life. Write each sentence in the correct column.

Fantasy	Reality

Tell a family member something new you learned in this unit.

Name _____   Date _____

Writing Workshop: Write a
Descriptive Essay

Read the passage. Then read each question on the next page and circle the correct answer.

The County Fair

(1) I love the county fair. (2) At the fair, I can see a rodeo.
(3) A cowboy rides on a big bull. (4) The bull jumps up and down.
(5) Everybody yells. (6) After a few seconds, the cowboy falls off.
(6) He lands on the ground in a clouds of dust. (7) Ouch!

(8) I like to ride the Ferris Wheel. (9) I get some sticky, blue cotton candy put on my seat belt, and the Ferris Wheel takes me high up in the cool air. (10) I can see hundreds of people. (11) Some people are playing games win big toys, and some are listening to a country music band. (12) Everybody has fun at the fair.

1. What is the BEST way to combine sentences 4 and 5?

  A The bull jumps up and down, on everybody and yells.

  B The bull jumps up and down, and everybody yells the cowboy.

  C The bull jumps up and down, and everybody yells.

  D The bull jumps up and down, or everybody is yelling.

2. What change, if any, should be made in sentence 6?

  A Change *clouds* to *cloud*

  B Change *lands* to *you land*

  C Change *He* to *It*

  D Make no change

3. What change, if any, should be made in sentence 8?

  A Change *ride* to *riding*

  B Change *ride* to *rode*

  C Change *ride* to *rides*

  D Make no change

4. What is the BEST way to revise sentence 9?

  A Add a comma after *candy*

  B Add a comma after *on*

  C Add a comma after *Wheel*

  D No revision is needed.

5. What change, if any, should be made in sentence 11?

  A Change *win* to *won*

  B Change *win* to *to win*

  C Change *win* to *wins*

  D Make no change

Name _____ Date _____

Fluency

Use with Student Book page 65.

How fast are you? Use a clock. Read the text about _The Star Llama_. How long did it take you? Write your time in the chart. Read three times.

The Star Llama is the story of a young Inca boy who had no	14
family except for an old llama. Every day the boy and llama	26
walked, and every night they went to sleep under the stars.	37
One evening the llama died. The boy was very sad but took	49
comfort from the stars in the sky. One night the sky was filled	62
with a bright light. The star took the shape of the llama and	75
drank from the stream. When the llama jumped back into the	86
sky, soft and warm llama wool fell to earth. The boy sold the	99
wool and bought a house. He never forgot the old llama.	110

My Times

Learning Checklist

Word Study and Phonics

☐ Short Vowels

☐ Endings: *-s, -es, -ed*

☐ Long Vowels with Silent *e*

Strategies

☐ Reread for Details

☐ Fantasy and Reality

☐ Preview

Grammar

☐ Simple Present

☐ Simple Past: *be* verbs

☐ Simple Past: Regular Verbs

Writing

☐ Describe an Animal

☐ Describe Yourself

☐ Describe a Place You Visit

☐ Writing Workshop: Write a Descriptive Essay

Listening and Speaking

☐ Play a Description Guessing Game

Name _____ Date _____

Test Preparation

Use with Student Book pages 66–67.

Read the selection. Then choose the correct words to fill in the blanks.

I spent a week at the Old River Ranch last summer. Mr. and Mrs. Lopez treated us like we really worked there. They had animals like horses, cattle, chickens, and pigs on the ranch. Each morning, we woke up very early to help feed all the ____1____. I liked watching the ____2____ colt the best. It was days-old and still very wobbly. It looked a little nervous. The colt stood right next to its mother so she could ____3____ it. I hope I can spend some ____4____ on a ranch again. It was great!

1.

  A geese

  B livestock

  C chicks

  D colts

2.

  F warm

  G young

  H feral

  J banned

3.

  A protect

  B shimmer

  C capture

  D recover

4.

  F work

  G food

  H time

  J money

Read the selection. Then choose the correct words to fill in the blanks.

Each summer, my family and I go to the ____1____ almost every weekend. We go there early in the morning. My parents lie down on their beach towels, under a big beach umbrella. My sister and I run on the beach. The ____2____ is hot under my feet. We play in the ____3____, too. By 10:00, there are hundreds of people on the beach. We eat lunch there, too. Sometimes we buy ice cream for a snack. I like to watch the ____4____ going up and down. My whole family loves the beach.

1.
- **A** beach
- **B** forest
- **C** city
- **D** trees

2.
- **F** water
- **G** sand
- **H** waves
- **J** sun

3.
- **A** lunch
- **B** castles
- **C** leaves
- **D** water

4.
- **F** towels
- **G** waves
- **H** snacks
- **J** beaches

Name _____ Date _____

Key Words

Use with Student Book pages 74–75.

volcano
lava
crater
erupts
ash

A. **Choose the word that *best* completes each sentence. Write the word.**

1. The _____ in the air made it hard to breathe.

2. It is a bad idea to live on a _____.

3. The largest _____ on the moon is over 1,300 miles across.

4. Hot _____ poured down the side of the volcano.

5. When the volcano _____ it hurt my ears.

B. **Choose the word that *best* matches the meaning of the underlined words. Write the word.**

6. When the smoke, fire, and rocks <u>escape</u> it makes a lot of noise.

   _____

7. Martin explored the <u>round hole in the ground</u>.

   _____

8. Dad says to stay away from the <u>mountain with a hole in the top</u>.

   _____

9. <u>Hot liquid</u> comes out of volcanoes. _____

10. The logs in our campfire will turn to <u>soft gray powder</u>.

   _____

Academic Words

Use with Student Book page 76.

consist of
evidence
similar

A. **Choose the word that *best* completes each sentence. Write the word.**

1. Cookies mostly _____ flour, sugar, and eggs.

2. What _____ do you have to support your claim?

3. Everyone thinks we are brothers because we look _____.

B. **Choose the word that *best* matches the meaning of the underlined words. Write the word.**

4. All <u>signs</u> of life were buried under the lava. _____

5. The exhibit <u>includes</u> gold and silver jewelry found at the site.

_____

6. Two mountains could look <u>almost identical</u> from far away.

_____

C. **Answer the questions.**

7. Name a famous person you think you look **similar** to. Why?

_____

_____

8. What activities does your school day **consist of**?

_____

_____

 **Write a question using each key word. Ask a family member to answer your questions.**

Name _____ Date _____

Word Study: Pronunciation of Ending -*ed*

Use with Student Book page 77.

> Writers add **-ed** to a regular verb to show something happened in the past.

Check the boxes that tell about each word when *-ed* is added. The first one is done for you.

	-*ed* sounds like *d*	-*ed* sounds like *t*	-*ed* adds a syllable
1. melted	☑	☐	☑
2. jumped	☐	☐	☐
3. called	☐	☐	☐
4. wanted	☐	☐	☐
5. looked	☐	☐	☐
6. barked	☐	☐	☐
7. tasted	☐	☐	☐
8. pulled	☐	☐	☐
9. needed	☐	☐	☐
10. missed	☐	☐	☐

Home-School Connection Write sentences in the past tense using three of the words above. Share your sentences with a family member.

43

Comprehension: Vesuvius Erupts!

Use with Student Book pages 78–81.

Answer the questions about the reading.

Recall

1. What was the weather like the morning Mount Vesuvius erupted?

_____

2. Why did roofs collapse after Mount Vesuvius erupted?

_____

3. How many people were able to escape?

_____

Comprehend

4. What did the ash and smoke do to the city of Pompeii and the people who lived there?

_____

_____

Analyze

5. Why do you think some people stayed in the city after the eruption?

_____

_____

_____

Name _____ Date _____

Reader's Companion

Use with Student Book pages 78–81.

Vesuvius Erupts!

About 2,000 people stayed in the city. Some chose to stay. Others were trapped. All of them died. But 20,000 people were able to escape.

In less than two days, ash and rocks buried the city. Heavy rain made the ash hard like cement. Pompeii stayed buried for almost 1,700 years!

In about 1750, the King of Naples ordered workers to uncover Pompeii.

Use What You Know

List three things you know about volcanoes.

1. _____

2. _____

3. _____

Genre MARK the TEXT

Underline one sentence that tells you how many people escaped.

Reading Strategy MARK the TEXT

Circle the title. What does it tell you about the reading?

Use the Strategy

How did making predictions help you to understand the passage?

_____

_____

_____

Retell It!

Retell this passage as if you are a news reporter living in Pompeii at the time of the eruption.

_____

_____

_____

_____

Reader's Response

Think about Pompeii at the time Vesuvius erupts. What would you do to stay safe?

_____

_____

_____

Home-School Connection   Retell the passage to a family member.

Learning Strategies: Sequence of Events

Use with Student Book pages 84–85.

Read the passage.

Jose's Afternoon

It was a sunny afternoon. Jose sat at his desk. He looked up at the clock. The clock said it was two o'clock. School would soon be over. Jose wanted to be outside. Suddenly, the bell rang. Jose ran out of school. He saw his friends. Together they ran to the park. They played soccer for an hour. Jose scored a goal. His team won the game. After the game, Jose walked home.

List the story events in the correct sequence. Write 1, 2, 3, 4, and 5 on the lines.

_____ He saw that school was almost over.

_____ His team won the game.

_____ Jose played soccer for an hour.

_____ The school bell rang.

_____ Jose sat at his desk and looked at the clock.

Home-School Connection Write three sentences that tell what Jose did next. Share your sentences with a family member.

Grammar: Irregular Past Verbs

Use with Student Book pages 86–87.

Review these **common irregular verbs** from the reading.

become ➔ **became**	fall ➔ **fell**	make ➔ **made**
begin ➔ **began**	find ➔ **found**	rise ➔ **rose**
blow ➔ **blew**	give ➔ **gave**	run ➔ **ran**
choose ➔ **chose**	have ➔ **had**	sing ➔ **sang**

Write the correct past tense form of the verb in parentheses to complete each sentence.

Example: (make) The eruption <u>made</u> the ground shake.

1. (blow) The wind _____ the leaves.

2. (choose) I _____ the book about Italy.

3. (run) He _____ all the way home.

4. (rise) The sun _____ over the bay.

5. (find) Workers _____ the city of Pompeii.

6. (begin) The volcano _____ to erupt.

7. (give) My mother _____ me a present.

8. (become) The sky suddenly _____ dark.

9. (sing) A group of musicians _____ a song.

10. (fall) Ash _____ from the sky.

Write five sentences about the eruption in Pompeii. Use irregular past verbs. Share your sentences with a family member.

Name _____ Date _____

Spelling: Past Tense Words with -ed

Use with Student Book pages 88–89.

Read each sentence. Use -ed to rewrite each verb in the past tense.

1. My dogs bark in the morning.

_____

2. Snow covers her doghouse.

_____

3. My brother and I watch the TV news.

_____

4. We wait for the weather report. _____

5. We play outside in the snow. _____

6. We like our snowman. _____

> ## SPELLING TIP
>
> Regular verbs that tell about actions in the past end in -ed. Make sure you add -ed to regular verbs when you write about the past.

Write about a snowy day. Tell what the kids did when the snow ended.

_____

_____

_____

_____

Home-School Connection Write a sentence for each of the spelling words. Show a family member how to pronounce the words.

Writing: Organize Ideas by Cause and Effect

Read the paragraph. Then read each question and circle the correct answer.

(1) The top of Mount Vesuvius blew off. (2) Smoke filled the air. (3) Ash fell from the sky, covering everything. (4) Within two days, Pompeii was buried. (5) Heavy rains fell. (6) The rainwater mixed with the ash, making it like wet cement. (7) The wet ash dried and hardened quickly. (8) Everything in Pompeii was stuck in the hardened ash. (9) The city stayed buried for hundreds of years. (10) Workers began covering the city in 1750. (11) The ash had preserved Pompeii! (12) People and things were exactly as they were at the time of the eruption. (13) It was frozen in time.

1. What is the BEST way to revise sentences 5, 6, and 7?
   A *Heavy rains fell and rainwater mixed with the ash, which quickly dried and hardened.*
   B *Then heavy rains fell, and the result was wet cement.*
   C *Heavy rains fell, and the rainwater mixed with the ash, making it like wet cement.*
   D No revision is needed.

2. What change, if any, should be made in sentence 10?
   A Change *in* to *during*
   B Change *covering* to *uncovering*
   C Change *Workers* to *Worker's*
   D Make no change

3. What is the BEST way to revise sentences 12 and 13?
   A *Positioned exactly as they were when they died, the people and things were left frozen in time.*
   B *Pompeii's people and things stayed exactly as they were at the time of the eruption, all frozen in time for all time.*
   C *People and things were frozen in time.*
   D No revision is needed.

Name _____ Date _____

Key Words

Use with Student Book pages 90–91.

| lightning |
| thunder |
| electricity |
| temperature |
| evaporate |

A. Choose the word that *best* completes each sentence. Write the word.

1. A bolt of _____ hit the tree.

2. Computers and TV sets need _____ to work.

3. Water will _____ before it turns into gas.

4. We were very cold because the _____ was low.

5. The loud _____ scared the dog so it hid under the bed.

B. Read each sentence. Write TRUE or FALSE.

6. A bicycle needs electricity to work. _____

7. When the temperature is high, many people go to the beach. _____

8. After you see lightning, you usually hear thunder. _____

9. Water will not evaporate if it boils. _____

10. The loud noise in the clouds sounded like a train. _____

Academic Words

Use with Student Book page 92.

appropriate
demonstrate
feature

A. Match each word with its definition. Write the letter of the correct answer.

1. appropriate _____

A a part that stands out

2. feature _____

B show how to do something

3. demonstrate _____

C fitting, suitable

B. Choose the word that best completes each sentence. Write the word.

4. The best _____ of our new car is the sunroof.

5. You can _____ static electricity by rubbing a balloon against your hair.

6. When it rains it's _____ to use an umbrella, except when there is lightning.

C. Answer the questions.

7. How does a cat **demonstrate** it's scared?

_____

_____

8. What's the best **feature** of your school?

_____

_____

 **Home-School Connection** Write a clue for each vocabulary word. Ask a family member to guess the answer.

Name _____ Date _____

Word Study: Compound Words

Use with Student Book page 93.

> Little words can be part of bigger words. Some bigger words are made of two little words put together.

A. Write the smaller words found in each compound word.

1. lightning _____

2. faster _____

3. unwelcome _____

4. playing _____

5. teacher _____

B. Read each word. Add another word or a word part to make a larger word.

6. some _____

7. talk _____

8. fun _____

9. light _____

10. good _____

Home-School Connection Make as many words as possible from the word *day* by adding words or word parts. Share your list with a family member.

Comprehension: Thunder and Lightning

Use with Student Book pages 94–97.

Answer the questions about the reading.

Recall

1. What is lightning?

_____

2. Why does lightning strike more in the summer than in the winter?

_____

3. What is thunder?

_____

Comprehend

4. What are the appropriate actions to take when you are outdoors during a thunderstorm?

_____

_____

Analyze

5. What helpful tips about staying safe during a thunderstorm do you think Emilio will include in his next letter to his grandmother?

_____

_____

_____

Name _____ Date _____

Reader's Companion

Use with Student Book pages 94–97.

Thunder and Lightning

Staying Safe in a Lightning Storm

1. Check if thunderstorms are in the forecast.

2. Find shelter in a strong building or in a car with a hard roof.

3. Do not stand under trees that are alone in the middle of a field. Do not stand under tall trees when there are shorter trees close by.

4. Do not stand near things that are made of metal.

Use What You Know

List three things you know about thunderstorms.

1. _____

2. _____

3. _____

Reading Strategy

MARK the TEXT

How do you know that this is an example of a how-to poster? Circle one feature of a how-to poster.

Comprehension Check

List three good places to put this poster.

1. _____

2. _____

3. _____

Use the Strategy

Where else have you seen a how-to poster? What did the poster teach or tell you to do?

_____

_____

_____

_____

Retell It!

Retell this passage as if you were caught in a thunderstorm. Tell how you followed these rules to stay safe.

_____

_____

_____

_____

Reader's Response

Write a list of safety rules to follow during a hurricane. Use what you read in the passage as a model.

_____

_____

_____

Retell the passage to a family member.

Learning Strategies: Compare Genres

Use with Student Book pages 98–99.

Read each passage. Mark an X next to the correct genre. Explain the features that helped you to decide.

1. Dear Aunt Peggy,

How are you? I am fine. Space Camp is fun! Every day I learn something new. Maybe some day I will visit the Space Station.

Love, Bobbie

_____ Informational Article

_____ How-To Poster

_____ Letter

_____

_____

2. Benjamin Franklin was a scientist. He learned about electricity. He also was a great leader. Franklin helped write the Declaration of Independence. He also helped start the first public library. Today, Americans thank Benjamin Franklin for his work in science, politics, and literature.

_____ Informational Article

_____ How-To Poster

_____ Letter

_____

_____

Write a short letter to a friend. Explain to a family member why your letter is different from an informational article and a how-to poster.

Grammar: Imperatives and Time-Order Transitions

Use with Student Book pages 100–101.

Review the common **imperative** forms and **time-order** expressions.

> An imperative is a sentence that gives a command. A command is a statement that tells a person or a group what to do or how to act.

A. Underline the sentences that are commands.

Example: <u>Listen to me!</u>

1. Get the phone!

3. Stephan, answer the phone.

2. Did you hear the phone ring?

4. Call me.

B. Unscramble the following phrases so they make a complete sentence.

Example: then come / your homework, / eat dinner / first, finish
<u>First, finish your homework, then come eat dinner.</u>

5. then go to bed / watch your television show, / as soon as you finish dinner,

_____

6. grades improve / home, until your / after school you will / come straight

_____

Write five commands that a school bus driver might use while working. Show your commands to a family member.

Name _____ Date _____

Spelling: Word Parts

Use with Student Book pages 102–103.

A. Draw a line between each word in Column A and a word or word part in Column B to make a new word. Then write the new word on the line.

SPELLING TIP

Word parts like *-ly* and *-y* form a new word.

Use a dictionary to learn how word parts change a word's meaning.

	Column A	Column B
1. _____	quick	body
2. _____	out	ly
3. _____	some	y
4. _____	cloud	side

B. Complete each word using a word part.

ing	un	under	yard

5. build _____   **7.** back _____

6. _____ ground   **8.** _____ tie

 Write a sentence using one of the answer words.

_____

Home-School Connection Use each of the word parts to write another word. Show your words to a family member.

59

Copyright © by Pearson Education, Inc.

Writing: Explain How to Do Something

Read the paragraph. Then read each question and circle the correct answer.

Make a Guitar

(1) Glue four toothpicks on the lid. (2) Space the toothpicks evenly between the hole and the other end of the lid. (3) Cut a hole near one end of a shoe box lid. (4) Slide the two thickest rubber bands around the shoe box, so they go across the hole in the lid. (5) Finally, slide the two thinnest rubber bands around the box in the same way. (6) Then slide the pencil under the four rubber bands. (7) Move the pencil at the very end of the box near the hole you cut. (8) Now play the guitar by plucking the rubber bands.

1. What change, if any, should be made with sentences 2 and 3?

   A Move sentence 2 to the beginning of the paragraph.

   B Move sentence 3 to the beginning of the paragraph.

   C Move sentence 3 to follow sentence 1.

   D Make no change

2. What change, if any, should be made in sentence 3?

   A Add *First* at the beginning

   B Add *Then* at the beginning

   C Add *Secondly* at the beginning

   D Make no change

3. What change, if any, should be made in sentence 5?

   A Change *Finally, slide* to *Slide*

   B Change *two* to *three*

   C Change *Finally* to *Then*

   D Make no change

Name _____ Date _____

Key Words

Use with Student Book pages 104–105.

breeze
hurricane
shelter
bolt

A. Choose the word that *best* matches the meaning of the underlined words. Write the word.

1. The <u>storm with heavy wind and rain</u> pulled street

signs from the ground. _____

2. We saw <u>a quick flash</u> of lightning during the storm.

_____

3. Your house is a good <u>safe place</u> when it rains.

_____

4. Did you feel the <u>soft wind</u> on your face? _____

B. Read each clue. Find the key word in the row of letters. Then circle the word.

5. spark of lightning   o n e s b t b o l t c a t u r n s h

6. gently moving air   d e r b r e e z e f h s t h u i r k

7. large, dangerous storm   o d h u r r i c a n e o o n i n g q

8. protected spot   z e r r f i s h e l t e r m s i t w

Academic Words

Use with Student Book page 106.

assistance

impact

major

A. Choose the word that *best* completes each sentence. Write the word.

1. Dial 9-1-1 if you need immediate _____ during an emergency.

2. During a hurricane, ocean waves can cause _____ flooding.

3. A teacher can have a big _____ on her students.

B. Choose the word that *best* matches the meaning of the underlined words.

4. His voice was the <u>most significant</u> reason everyone came to hear the choir sing.

5. The tutor offered him some <u>help</u> in understanding his homework.

6. My classmates <u>influence</u> how hard I work.

C. Answer the questions.

7. How do you spend the **major** part of your day?

_____

_____

8. Who do you go to for **assistance** with difficult homework?

_____

_____

 Use each of the vocabulary words in a sentence. Share your sentences with a family member.

Name _____ Date _____

Phonics: Digraphs *ch*, *sh*, *th*

Use with Student Book page 107.

> The letter pairs *ch*, *sh*, and *th* each have one sound.
> These letters can be anywhere in a word.

**Read each word. Write the word in the correct column of the chart.
The first one is done for you.**

beaches   catch   ~~chair~~
fishing   mother   shore
three   wash   with

Letters	Beginning	Middle	End
ch	1. _chair_	2. _____	3. _____
sh	4. _____	5. _____	6. _____
th	7. _____	8. _____	9. _____

Home-School Connection Think of one word to add to each box in the chart. Show your
words to a family member.

Comprehension: Hurricane!

Use with Student Book pages 108–113.

Answer the questions about the reading.

Recall

1. How did the narrator and his family find out that a hurricane was approaching?

   _____

2. Why did the narrator's father nail wood over the windows of the beach house?

   _____

3. Where did travelers stay during the storm?

   _____

Comprehend

4. Describe what the narrator saw during the car ride to the hotel.

   _____

   _____

Analyze

5. What kind of impact do you think this adventure had on the narrator's life?

   _____

   _____

   _____

Name _____   Date _____

Reader's Companion

Use with Student Book pages 108–113.

Hurricane!

A man ran toward us. He worked at a nearby hotel.

"Señor! Señorita!" he called. "A big storm is coming. You must leave the beach now!" He told us that a hurricane was approaching. Everyone had to go to a shelter.

"But the water is so nice," I said sadly.

"Hurricanes are dangerous. We must leave," Dad said.

Mom smiled to make me feel better. Just then, I felt a breeze. Suddenly, the wind grew stronger and sand flew all around the beach.

"Let's go!" Dad said.

Use What You Know

List three things you know about hurricanes.

1. _____

2. _____

3. _____

Reading Strategy

MARK the TEXT

Circle two examples in the passage that tell you about the setting.

Comprehension Check

MARK the TEXT

Someone ran over to the family on the beach. Underline the paragraph that tells you who this was.

Use the Strategy

What clues in the passage helped you understand what a hurricane is like?

_____

_____

_____

_____

Retell It!

Retell this passage as if you are a weather reporter. Tell people about the approaching hurricane.

_____

_____

_____

_____

Reader's Response

What would you do if a hurricane were coming?

_____

_____

_____

_____

Retell the passage to a family member.

Name _____ Date _____

Learning Strategies: Clues to Setting

Use with Student Book pages 114–115.

Read each story. Then answer the questions.

1. It was summer. The sand was very hot. The waves were tall. The breeze smelled salty. "Do you think the water is warm?" Jerry asked his friend. Caleb laughed. "There's only one way to find out."

Write two clues that tell where the story takes place.

_____

_____

Where are Jerry and Caleb?

_____

2. "There's nowhere to park," said Dad. Joanie looked around. The parking lot was filled with cars. "Look at all these shoppers," said Joanie. It was a rainy Saturday. People wanted to be inside. Joanie sighed. Dad said, "After we find a place to park, we'll go to your favorite stores."

Write two clues that tell where the story takes place.

_____

_____

Where are Dad and Joanie?

_____

 **Tell a family member about a storm you experienced, read about, or saw in a film. Include details about the setting.**

Grammar: Adjectives

Use with Student Book pages 116–117.

Review the different types of **adjectives** and their word order.

opinion	Her orange coat is **funny**.
size	She wore the **long** orange coat to school.
color	I like her **orange** coat.
material	She wears her **leather** coat on special occasions.
purpose	She calls her green coat a **gardening** jacket.

A. Complete each sentence by adding **adjectives** to describe each noun.

Example: I could not carry everything in my <u>small</u> backpack.

1. The breeze felt _____ just before it started to rain.

2. My dad said the _____ waves were because of the hurricane.

3. The _____ , _____ ball was his favorite.

B. Underline all the **adjectives** in the sentence, then write the type for each **adjective**.

Example: I could not carry everything in my <u>small</u> backpack. <u>size</u>

4. The water in the swimming pool was blue and inviting.

    _____

5. We broke the white glass vase by accident. _____

6. The older students take classes in the red brick building.

    _____

Write five sentences using the same noun. For each sentence, use different adjectives to describe the noun. Share your sentences with a family member.

Name _____   Date _____

Spelling: /k/ Sound

Use with Student Book pages 118–119.

Underline the word in each sentence that has the /k/ sound. Draw a box around the letter or letters that spell the /k/ sound. Then write the word.

1. Books are nice to read.

_____

2. Did you pick the flowers? _____

3. Would you like to play? _____

4. The water was as cold as ice. _____

✎   **Write a short story about a black cat that acts like a kangaroo.**

_____

_____

_____

Home-School Connection Think of two words for each /k/ sound spelled with *c*, *k*, and *ck*. Use each word in a sentence. Share your sentences with a family member.

Writing: Explain a Process

Read the selection. Then read each question and circle the correct answer.

(1) 1. In the first stage, a butterfly attaches a very tiny egg to a leaf or stem.

(2) 2. In the next stage, a long caterpillar develops. (3) It sheds its outer skin three or four times. (4) It has an interesting pattern of stripes on its body. (5) The caterpillar feeds and grows.

(6) 3. In the third stage a pupa, or chrysalis, develops it is wrapped in a tough green or brown outer case called a cocoon. (7) The pupa turns into a butterfly.

(8) 4. Finally, a beautiful butterfly leaves the cocoon. (9) This colorful butterfly will travel to new places.

1. What new order, if any, should sentences 3, 4, and 5 have?
   A New sentence order 5, 4, 3
   B New sentence order 4, 5, 3
   C New sentence order 3, 5, 4
   D Make no change

2. What change, if any, should be made in sentence 8?
   A Add *Secondly*, at the beginning
   B Add *Finally*, at the beginning
   C Add *Then* at the beginning
   D Make no change

3. What change, if any, should be made in sentence 6?
   A Change *develops it* to *develops. It*
   B Change *develops* to *developed*
   C Change *wrapped* to *wraped*
   D Make no change

Name _____ Date _____

Review

Use with Student Book pages 68–119.

A. Answer the questions after reading Unit 2. You can go back and reread to help find the answers.

1. Which question is not answered by the end of *Vesuvius Erupts!*? Circle the letter of the correct answer.

    A Why did the King of Naples have workers uncover Pompeii?

    B What fell from the sky after Mt. Vesuvius erupted?

    C How long did Pompeii stay buried under ash?

    D What caused the city of Pompeii to disappear?

2. Read these sentences from the story.

> Boom! Suddenly, the top of Mount Vesuvius blew off! Now the mountain had a crater.

What does *crater* mean? Circle the letter of the correct answer.

    A top   **C** explode

    B hole   **D** lava

3. Write a sentence telling what Pompeii was like after the eruption of Mt. Vesuvius.

_____

_____

4. Underline two words that tell you about the setting at the beginning of *Hurricane!*

> On our second day of vacation, I splashed in the sea. Mom and Dad sat on the shore. A strong breeze blew sand into my face.

5. Write the adjective in this sentence.

The waves were strong that day. _____

6. Circle the sentences that contain a verb in the past tense.

A The sky was dark.   **C** "Our vacation is ruined."

B Rain fell from the sky.   **D** It was the afternoon.

B. Read this passage from *Thunder and Lightning.* Then answer questions 7–9.

Lightning is a big flash of electricity. It is released during a storm. Thunder is the noise we hear when the air explodes.

7. Which word has the digraph *sh?* _____

8. Identify the genre of the passage.

A friendly letter   **B** how-to poster   **C** informational article

9. Look at the Venn diagram. Circle the sentence that is incorrect.

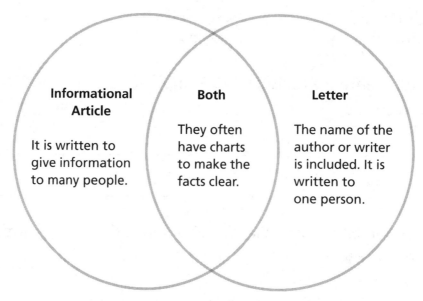

Informational Article

It is written to give information to many people.

Both

They often have charts to make the facts clear.

Letter

The name of the author or writer is included. It is written to one person.

Tell a family member something new you learned from this unit.

Name _____ Date _____

Writing Workshop: Write a How-to Essay

Read the passage. Then read each question on the next page and circle the correct answer.

Planning a Surprise Party

(1) To plan a surprise party for a friend, just follow this steps. (2) First, think of the time and place of the party. (3) Your friend must be free at that time.

(4) Next, invite people the party. (5) Make sure they knows it is a secret. (6) They must not tell your friend.

(7) First, ask someone to bring your friend to the party, but without saying it is a party. (8) They can come by bus or by train.

(9) Finally, the people at the party should turn out the lights and wait. (10) When the friend arrives, turn on the lights and yell, "Surprise!" (11) Have a great party!

1. What change, if any, should be made in sentence 1?
   A Change *this* to *these*
   B Change *follow* to *you follow*
   C Change a *friend* to *the friend*
   D Make no change

2. What change, if any, should be made in sentence 5?
   A Change *Make* to *Made*
   B Change *knows* to *know*
   C Change *it* to *them*
   D Make no change

3. What change, if any, should be made in sentence 7?
   A Change *First* to *After*
   B Change *First* to *Then after*
   C Change *First* to *After that*
   D Make no change

4. What is the BEST way to revise sentence 10?
   A When turn on the lights, the friend arrives, and yell, "Surprise!"
   B When the friend arrives, turn on the lights and "Yell, surprise!"
   C When the friend yells, "Surprise!" arrives, turn on the lights.
   D No revision is needed.

5. Which sentence does NOT belong in this story?
   A Sentence 3
   B Sentence 4
   C Sentence 6
   D Sentence 8

Name _____   Date _____

Fluency

Use with Student Book page 127.

How fast are you? Use a clock. Read the text about *Thunder and Lightning*. How long did it take you? Write your time in the chart. Read three times.

Thunder and Lightning explains what happens in the	8
sky to form lightning and thunder during storms.	16
Cold air makes the water vapor in clouds turn into	26
water drops or ice crystals. Each of these carries a tiny	37
bit of electricity. The electricity builds until lightning	45
suddenly flashes. Each bolt of lightning is five times	54
hotter than the sun.	58
Lightning heats the air around it so quickly that the	68
air explodes. Thunder is the loud noise we hear when	78
the air explodes. Light travels faster than sound. This	87
is why we see the lightning first and hear the thunder	98
later. Thunder usually happens five seconds after	105
we see the lightning flashes.	110

My Times

Learning Checklist

Word Study and Phonics

☐ Pronunciation of Ending *-ed*

☐ Compound Words

☐ Digraphs: *ch*, *sh*, *th*

Strategies

☐ Predict   ☐ Compare Genres

☐ Sequence of Events   ☐ Visualize Setting

☐ Identify Genre   ☐ Clues to Setting

Grammar

☐ Irregular Past Verbs

☐ Imperatives and Time-Order Transitions

☐ Adjectives

Writing

☐ Organize by Cause and Effect

☐ Explain How to Do Something

☐ Explain a Process

☐ Writing Workshop: Write a How-to Essay

Listening and Speaking

☐ Give a How-to Presentation

Name _____ Date _____

Test Preparation

Use with Student Book pages 128–129.

Read the selection. Then answer the questions.

(1) It stopped to rain in the Southwest in the summer of 1931. (2) Crops died. (3) There was nothing left to hold the dirt on the ground. (4) Then the dust storms begin. (5) It was called the Dust Bowl, and it lasted for 10 years. (6) There was dust everywhere. (7) There was dust in the food and in the water. (8) It is hard for animals and people to breathe. (9) Sometimes there was so much dust in the air, you couldn't see the sun. (10) The sky become so dark, it looked like night during the day.

1. What is the BEST way to revise sentence 1?
   A It stopped raining in the Southwest in the summer of 1931.
   B It stop rained in the Southwest in the summer of 1931.
   C It stop to rain in the Southwest in the summer of 1931.
   D No revision is needed.

2. What is the BEST way to revise sentence 4?
   F Then the dust storms end.
   G Then the dust storms begun.
   H Then the dust storms began.
   J No revision is needed.

3. What revision, if any, is necessary in sentence 8?
   A It was hard for animals and people to breathe.
   B It were hard for animals and people to breathe.
   C It are hard for animals and people to breathe.
   D No revision is needed.

4. What change, if any, should be made in sentence 10?
   F Change *looked* to **look**.
   G Change *become* to **became**.
   H Change *become* to **were**.
   J Make no change.

Read the selection. Then answer the questions.

(1) In late December 2009, a big winter storm hitted a large part of the United States. (2) The storm did bring a lot of snow to Texas, as well as many other states. (3) The town of Post, Texas reported 9 inches of snow from the storm.

(4) The storm was very large. It stretched from Canada, all the way down to Dallas, Texas. (5) The Dallas area seen its first "white Christmas" since 1929. (6) The storm brought many problems, too. (7) Airports were closed and there were many traffic accidents. (8) There were also several tornadoes, including one near Longview, and another near Lufkin, Texas.

1. What revision is necessary in sentence 1?

  A In late December 2009, a big winter storm was hit a large part of the United States.

  B In late December 2009, a big winter storm hit a large part of the United States.

  C In late December 2009, a big winter storm hits a large part of the United States.

  D No revision is needed.

2. What is the BEST way to revise sentence 2?

  F The storm brought a lot of snow to Texas, as well as many other states.

  G The storm brings a lot of snow to Texas, as well as many other states.

  H The storm was bringing a lot of snow to Texas, as well as many other states.

  J No revision is needed.

3. What is the BEST way to revise sentence 5?

  A The Dallas area saw its first "white Christmas" since 1929.

  B The Dallas area did see its first "white Christmas" since 1929.

  C The Dallas area is seeing its first "white Christmas" since 1929.

  D No revision is needed.

4. What change, if any, should be made in sentence 7?

  F Change *were* to **are**.

  G Change *closed* to **closer**.

  H Change *were* to **was**.

  J Make no change.

Name _____ Date _____

Key Words

Use with Student Book pages 136–137.

tidbit
mischief
nonsense
duty
satisfied
council

A. Match each word with its definition. Write the letter of the correct answer.

1. satisfied _____ **A** a small piece of something

2. duty _____ **B** something you have to do

3. nonsense _____ **C** happy with how things are

4. tidbit _____ **D** something that is silly

B. Choose the word that *best* completes each sentence. Write the word.

5. When you act silly, everything you say is _____!

6. It is everybody's _____ to obey the law.

7. The government _____ meets in Town Hall every Monday.

8. You will get in trouble if you make _____.

9. Julie was _____ with her good grades.

10. We have an interesting _____ of news to tell you.

Academic Words

Use with Student Book page 138.

emerge
react
respond

A. Choose the word that best completes each sentence. Write the word.

1. It was his duty to _____ immediately to a call for help.

2. Baby chicks _____ from their eggs after about four weeks.

3. The doctor gently taps your knee to test how you _____ .

B. Choose the word that *best* matches the meaning of the underlined words.

4. He <u>answers</u> only if you call him by his nickname. _____

5. My favorite flowers normally <u>appear</u> at the end of summer.

   _____

6. When someone throws a ball at me I <u>act</u> quickly. _____

C. Answer the questions.

7. Describe what dolphins look like when they **emerge** from the water.

   _____

   _____

8. How do you **react** to a surprise?

   _____

   _____

Think of another question for each key word. Share your questions with a family member.

Name _____ Date _____

Phonics: Long Vowel Pairs

Use with Student Book page 139.

> Two vowels together are a **vowel pair**. Usually, the first vowel in the pair has a long vowel sound. The sound of the second vowel is usually silent.

Long *a*	Long *e*	Long *i*	Long *o*	Long *u*
f<u>ai</u>l, b<u>ay</u>	n<u>ee</u>d	sk<u>ie</u>s	r<u>oa</u>d, f<u>oe</u>	cl<u>ue</u>, s<u>ui</u>t

A. Write the vowel sound in each word. Then circle the letters that spell that sound. The first one is done for you.

1. d(a y) _____ long a _____

2. g o e s _____

3. b l u e _____

4. f e e t _____

5. t i e d _____

6. l o a f _____

7. r a i n _____

8. f r u i t _____

B. Read each clue. Use a vowel pair to make a word with a long vowel sound.

9. it sails on water   b _____ _____ t

10. a month of the year   M _____ _____

11. can hold things together   g l _____ _____

12. they are baked with apples p _____ _____ s

Home-School Connection Write another word for each vowel pair in the chart. Show your words to a family member.

Comprehension:
Why Mosquitoes Buzz in People's Ears

Use with Student Book pages 140–145.

Answer the questions about the reading.

Recall

1. What did Mosquito try to tell Turtle?

_____

2. What did Mouse do when she saw Snake?

_____

3. Why did Owl forget to hoot?

_____

Comprehend

4. Why was Lion mad at Mosquito?

_____

_____

Analyze

5. In what ways did Lion show he was the leader of the forest?

_____

_____

_____

Name _____   Date _____

Reader's Companion

Use with Student Book pages 140–145.

Why Mosquitoes Buzz in People's Ears

Just then, Turtle walked by.

"Turtle!" Lion roared. "Are you Snake's friend?"

"What?" Turtle removed the leaves from her ears. "Yes, I am Snake's friend."

"Then why didn't you speak when Snake said hello?" asked Lion.

"I did not hear him," said Turtle. "Mosquito gossips, so I put leaves in my ears."

"All this mischief started with you, Mosquito," the angry lion said. "You may never talk again."

All the animals were satisfied, but not Mosquito. Even today mosquitoes want to talk. But all they can do is buzzzzz!

Use What You Know

List three reasons it's a bad idea to gossip.

1. _____

2. _____

3. _____

Genre

Underline the sentences that tell you this is a pourquoi tale.

Reading Strategy

Lion asked Turtle a question. Circle the sentence that tells what Turtle did next.

Use the Strategy

How did paying attention to the events in the plot of the story help you understand the passage?

_____

_____

_____

Retell It!

Retell this passage as if you are one of the characters in the tale.

_____

_____

_____

_____

Reader's Response

What did this passage teach you about gossip?

_____

_____

_____

Retell the passage to a family member.

Learning Strategies: Sequence of Events

Use with Student Book pages 146–147.

Read the passage. Then number the events in the order in which they occurred in the passage. The first one is done for you.

Irving

Irving was a snail. He was growing too big for his little shell. One morning he decided to find a new home.

On the street, Irving saw a small can. He climbed inside. "This house is too big!" he thought.

The next day, Irving found a teacup. "This home looks perfect," he thought. But the teacup had a big crack. "If it rains, I will get wet."

On the third day, Irving saw a store. "I can't find a home. But maybe I can buy one," he thought. Irving crossed the street. "Do you sell homes?" he asked the store owner.

The store owner smiled. "We sell shells," he said.

_____ Irving climbed inside a small can.

_____ Irving saw a store.

___1___ Irving was too big for his shell.

_____ The store owner said he sold shells.

_____ Irving decided to find a new home.

_____ Irving found a cracked teacup.

Write five sentences telling what you did on your last birthday. Be sure to write the events in the order in which they happened. Share your sentences with a family member.

Grammar: Singular and Plural Nouns

Use with Student Book pages 148–149.

Review the forms of **singular and plural nouns**.

desk ➡	desks	fox ➡	fox**es**	party ➡	part**ies**	
toy ➡	toys	potato ➡	potato**es**	radio ➡	radios	
life ➡	li**ves**	wolf ➡	wol**ves**	tooth ➡	**teeth**	

Rewrite each sentence. Change the *subject* of each sentence from a singular noun to a plural noun. Make any changes necessary to correct subject-verb agreement.

Example: The race is in the fall.

The races are in the fall.

1. The dog swims in the lake.

_____

2. His story is always exciting.

_____

3. The knife is sharp and dangerous.

_____

4. The bus to the city leaves early.

_____

5. The factory makes toys.

_____

Write five sentences with plural nouns not used in the exercise above. Make sure the verbs agree with your plural nouns. Share your sentences with a family member.

Name _____ Date _____

Spelling: Words with Difficult Spellings

Use with Student Book pages 150–151.

Look at each pair of words. Circle the word that is spelled correctly.

SPELLING TIP

In a notebook, write words you have trouble spelling. Study the words until they become easier to spell.

1. annoy   annoi

2. rok   rock

3. jumped   jumpt

4. tallist   tallest

5. gossip   gossyp

6. dangeris   dangerous

7. nonsense   nonesence

8. leaves   leeves

 Use three of the words to write a short story about an animal that likes to get into mischief.

_____

_____

_____

_____

_____

Home-School Connection Make a list of three words you want to know how to spell. Work with a family member to find those words in a dictionary to check their spellings.

Writing: Retell a Familiar Story

Read the story. Then read each question and circle the correct answer.

The Fox and the Crow

(1) One morning a black crow sit in a tree with many branches. (2) The crow held a piece of cheese in its beak. (3) Soon a fox walked by. (4) The hungry fox loved cheese. (5) But the crow did not like foxes, so she flew to a very high tree branch. (6) The smart fox called up to the crow. (7) He said she was more beautiful than any of the other crows. (8) But could she sing too? (9) Now, the proud crow was also a show-off she opened her beak very wide and sang for the fox. (10) Of course the cheese fell straight down and the fox ate it.

1. What change, if any, should be made in sentence 1?
    A Change *branches* to *branchs*
    B Change *sit* to *sat*
    C Change *sit* to *sitting*
    D Make no change

2. Which sentence could BEST be added after sentence 6?
    A The fox knew exactly what it would take to succeed.
    B The fox thought he had a plan.
    C The fox had a plan.
    D Make no change

3. What change, if any, should be made in sentence 9?
    A Change *show-off she* to *show-off? She*
    B Change *show-off she* to *show-off. She*
    C Change *sang* to *was singing*
    D Make no change

Name _____ Date _____

Key Words

Use with Student Book pages 152–153.

> fine
> whisk
> stitches
> stroke
> bare
> wink

A. **Choose the word that *best* completes each sentence. Write the word.**

1. I covered the _____ walls with pictures and photos.

2. My dad smiled proudly and said, "You wrote a

   _____ story."

3. When I tell a joke, I _____ and smile.

4. She had only a second to _____ away all the old newspapers.

5. This torn sock just needs a few _____.

6. Cinderella had to be home at the _____ of midnight.

B. **Read each sentence. Circle the word that correctly completes the sentence.**

7. This beautiful painting is a (stroke / fine) piece of art.

8. People sometimes (wink / whisk) when they say something funny.

9. We went to the supermarket because the kitchen shelves were almost (fine / bare).

10. Just a few more (whisk / stitches) and I'll stop sewing.

Academic Words

Use with Student Book page 154.

appreciate
benefit
infer

A. Write the word that *best* matches the definition.

1. To value something or someone. _____

2. To interpret evidence and come to a conclusion. _____

3. To be useful to someone. _____

B. Choose the word that *best* completes each sentence. Write the word.

4. We can _____ she ate the cake because of the crumbs on her dress.

5. I hope he will _____ the opportunity to see the Grand Canyon.

6. You _____ from living near school because you get home earlier.

C. Answer the questions.

7. What do you most **appreciate** about your family?

_____

_____

8. How do you **benefit** from being with your classmates?

_____

_____

 Write a second answer for each question. Share your answers with a family member.

90

Copyright © by Pearson Education, Inc.

Name _____   Date _____

Phonics: Vowel Pair: *ea*

Use with Student Book page 155.

> The **vowel pair** *ea* can have two sounds—the long *e* sound, as in *each*, and the short *e* sound, as in *head*.

A. Check the box that tells which vowel sound each word has.

	long *e* sound	short *e* sound
1. ready	☐	☐
2. neat	☐	☐
3. mean	☐	☐
4. heavy	☐	☐
5. please	☐	☐

B. Read each clue. Fill in the letters to complete the answer. In the box, write S if the word has the short *e* sound and L if it has the long *e* sound.

6. you need this to make a sandwich   _____ _____ e a _____ ☐

7. birds have these   _____ e a _____ _____ ☐

8. you do this while you sleep   _____ _____ e a _____ ☐

Get a newspaper or magazine article. Underline the words that have the short *e* vowel sound spelled *ea*. Draw a box around the words that have the long *e* vowel sound spelled *ea*. Show your work to a family member.

91

Comprehension:
The Shoemakers and the Elves

Use with Student Book pages 156–163.

Answer the questions about the reading.

Recall

1. Why doesn't Lumkin want to play a trick on the shoemakers?

_____

2. Why are Diego and Amelia worried?

_____

3. Where do Diego and Amelia put the shoes that the elves made?

_____

Comprehend

4. How do the elves react when they open the gifts?

_____

_____

Analyze

5. How can helping others benefit you?

_____

_____

Name _____ Date _____

Reader's Companion

Use with Student Book pages 156–163.

The Shoemakers and the Elves

Lumkin: Let's play a trick on them!

Pixie: No, Lumkin. I think we have had enough fun for one day. We need a warm place to rest.

Lumkin: You're right. I don't want to get chased out of another house. I'm cold.

Pixie: [She looks in the window again.] Those people look tired.

Lumkin: And their shelves look bare. The shoemakers have nothing to sell.

Use What You Know

List two ways Lumkin and Pixie helped the shoemakers.

1. _____

2. _____

Reading Strategy

MARK the TEXT

Circle the sentence that gives information about what season it might be.

Comprehension Check

MARK the TEXT

The elves say the shoemakers have nothing to sell. Underline the sentence that tells you how they know that.

Use the Strategy

How did making inferences help you understand this passage?

_____

_____

_____

Retell It!

Retell this passage as if it is a fairy tale. Start with the phrase
"Once upon a time…"

_____

_____

_____

_____

Reader's Response

What lesson did you learn from the passage?

_____

_____

_____

Retell the passage to a family member.

Name _____ Date _____

Learning Strategies: Infer and Predict

Use with Student Book pages 164–165.

Read the passage. Use what the author has told you to answer the questions. Write a complete sentence for each answer.

The Picnic

Ashley, Tawana, and Gina liked being together. So they planned a weekend picnic. Each girl would bring something on Saturday. They all decided to bring their favorite games.

Ashley wanted to bake an apple pie. Tawana wanted to make a salad. Gina said she would buy lemonade at the store.

On Saturday Ashley looked out the window. Dark clouds were in the sky. Suddenly, the phone rang. It was Tawana. She said, "Ashley, I have some bad news!"

1. How do you know Ashley, Tawana, and Gina are friends?

_____

2. How do you know the girls like to play games?

_____

3. How do you know Ashley and Tawana like to cook?

_____

4. How do you know Saturday's weather is bad?

_____

What will happen the next time the three girls go on a picnic? Write three sentences that show your predictions. Share your sentences with a family member.

Grammar: Possessives

Use with Student Book pages 166–167.

Review the forms of **possessive nouns**.

the school**'s** playground	the oxen**'s** horns.	the cars**'** tires
the boy**'s** watch	the geese**'s** wings.	the stories**'** lesson

Rewrite each phrase to make the nouns show possession.

Example: the strokes of the pen

<u>the pen's strokes</u>

1. the benefits of friendship

_____

2. the colors of the shoes

_____

3. the length of the pool

_____

4. the tools of the carpenter

_____

5. the smell of the cakes and pie

_____

 **Write five sentences using singular and plural possessives. Share your sentences with a family member.**

Name _____ Date _____

Spelling: Vowel Pairs with a Long Vowel Sound

Use with Student Book pages 168–169.

Each word below has a long vowel sound spelled *ai, ay, ea,* or *oa*. Add a letter to complete each word. Then write the word.

1. d a _____   _____

2. r _____ a d   _____

3. r a _____ n   _____

4. l _____ a v e   _____

5. s _____ y   _____

6. c l e _____ n   _____

7. p _____ i d   _____

8. t o _____ s t   _____

Use three of the words to write a dialogue between two farm workers.

_____

_____

_____

_____

Home-School Connection Think of two more words for each of the vowel pairs. Use each word in a sentence. Show your sentences to a family member.

Writing: Write a Friendly Letter

Read the letter. Then read each question and circle the correct answer.

(1) 32 First Avenue
(2) Philadelphia PA
(3) October 8, 2011

(4) Dear Rosetta,
(5) Last Saturday my dog Sam was in a neighborhood pet show at logan Park. (6) Many of our neighbors' pets were in the show, too. (7) People brung their dogs, cats, rabbits, birds, and fish. (8) I didn't think most of the animals would get along. (9) But they did—most of the time! (10) Then, in the middle of a contest, Sam's collar fell off and he raced around the park. (11) I guess he won't win prizes for being well behaved. (12) It didn't matter. (13) It was a wonderful day! (14) Write soon.

(15) Love, Kate

1. What change, if any, should be made in sentence 2?
   A Spell out the name of the state.
   B Take out the name of the city.
   C Add a comma after the name of the city.
   D Make no change

2. What change, if any, should be made in sentence 5?
   A Change *logan* to *Logan*
   B Change *dog Sam* was to *dog, Sam was*
   C Change *neighborhood* to *neighborhod*
   D Make no change

3. What change, if any, should be made in sentence 7?
   A Change *their* to *our*
   B Change *brung* to *brought*
   C Change *People* to *Everyone*
   D Make no change

Name _____ Date _____

Key Words
Use with Student Book pages 170–171.

| mighty |
| sledgehammer |
| machine |
| boasted |
| sputter |

A. Choose the word that _best_ completes each sentence. Write the word.

1. The only way to produce large amounts of clothing in a short period of time is to use a _____.

2. He had to use all his strength to swing the _____ to break through the heavy brick wall.

3. The thunderstorm brought heavy rain and _____ winds to the whole county.

4. The engine of the lawn mower began to shake and _____ just before it stopped working.

5. The proud fisherman _____ about catching the largest fish of the day.

B. Read the pairs of sentences. One sentence makes sense. The other is silly. Put a line through the sentence that is silly.

6. Many families use a machine to wash and dry their clothes.
Many families use a machine to get dressed in the morning.

7. A sledgehammer is a useful tool for fixing eyeglasses.
A sledgehammer is a useful tool for breaking down large rocks.

8. Only a mighty opponent had a chance against the world champions.
Only a mighty opponent had a chance against the last place team.

9. The boy boasted about the crushing defeat of his favorite team.
The boy boasted about the winning record of his favorite team.

Academic Words

Use with Student Book page 172.

anticipate
display
scenario

A. Choose the word that *best* completes each sentence. Write the word.

1. The contest allowed her to _____ her math skills.

2. He imagined a _____ in which his favorite team could win.

3. He didn't _____ that her train would arrive early.

B. Choose the word that *best* matches the meaning of the underlined words. Write the word.

4. The divers <u>show off</u> the treasures. _____

5. I <u>expect</u> the test will be hard, so I will study tonight. _____

6. I described a <u>situation</u> where it was OK to eat ice cream for dinner.
_____

C. Answer the questions.

7. Briefly describe a **scenario** in which you could go to the moon.

_____

_____

8. What do you **anticipate** will happen to you next year?

_____

_____

 **Write a question using each academic word. Ask a family member to answer your questions.**

Name _____ Date _____

Word Study: Synonyms and Antonyms

Use with Student Book page 173.

> **Synonyms** are words that mean the same or almost the same thing.
>
> **Antonyms** are words that have opposite meanings.

A. Write the synonym for each underlined word.

jump	loud	laugh	shut	seats

1. The crowd was very <u>noisy</u>. _____

2. All of the <u>chairs</u> were lined up in a row. _____

3. Frogs and rabbits can <u>hop</u>. _____

4. I'll <u>close</u> the window if it gets too hot. _____

5. Funny movies make me <u>giggle</u>. _____

B. Match each word with its antonym. Write the letter of the correct answer.

6. end _____   **a.** sad

7. freezing _____   **b.** far

8. happy _____   **c.** begin

9. near _____   **d.** long

10. short _____   **e.** boiling

 **Home-School Connection** Think of three synonym pairs and three antonym pairs. Use each word in a sentence. Show your sentences to a family member.

Comprehension: John Henry and the Machine

Use with Student Book pages 174–177.

Answer the questions about the reading.

Recall

1. What could John Henry do as a baby that no other baby could do?

_____

2. Who did John Henry work for when he grew up?

_____

3. What did a stranger bring to town?

_____

Comprehend

4. Why was John Henry so happy working for the railroad?

_____

_____

Analyze

5. Why did the stranger want to prove that his machine was more powerful than ten men?

_____

_____

Name _____ Date _____

Reader's Companion

Use with Student Book pages 174–177.

John Henry and the Machine

The stranger boasted that his drilling machine could do more work than ten men.

"Impossible!" John Henry cried. "No machine can do more work than I can."

The stranger challenged John Henry to a contest. He wanted to prove what his machine could do.

He pointed to a wall of rock. "Let's see who can drill through that!" Then he started his machine. John Henry raised his hammer.

John Henry and the machine worked. They worked all day and night. They each broke through the thick wall, one rock at a time.

Use What You Know

List three things you know about John Henry.

1. _____

2. _____

3. _____

Comprehension Check

How does John Henry feel about his ability to work hard? Underline the words that tell you the answer.

MARK the TEXT

Reading Strategy

MARK the TEXT

What do you know about the main character of the passage? Circle two words that tell you something about that character.

Use the Strategy

What words helped you learn more about the character in the passage?

_____

_____

_____

Retell It!

Retell this passage as if you are John Henry explaining what happened.

_____

_____

_____

_____

Reader's Response

Do you like stories like the one about John Henry? Why or why not?

_____

_____

_____

Home-School Connection Retell the passage to a family member.

Name _____   Date _____

Learning Strategies: Identify Character

Use with Student Book pages 180–181.

Read the passage. Look for clues that tell you about the character.

I Don't Want to Be Extinct!

The jungle where I live
May be gone one day.
It is getting very small.

I'm a gorilla from Africa.
I eat plants and leaves and ants.
I'm very big. I'm six feet tall.

And I am asking you
My caring human friend
To help to save us all.

1. Where does the main character live? _____

_____

2. What does the main character look like? _____

_____

3. What does the main character eat? _____

_____

4. What does the main character want? _____

_____

Write three sentences about an interesting character in a book you read. Show your sentences to a family member.

Grammar: Quotations

Use with Student Book pages 182–183.
Review the rules for **quotations**.

> "Would you like me to read you a story?" Grandmother asked.
>
> "Your report is due on Friday," the teacher said, "and please read chapter 5 for Monday."
>
> My brother likes the cowboy song "Goodbye Old Paint."

Rewrite the sentences using quotation marks. Be sure to use proper spacing and punctuation.

Example: Read the three cowboy stories the teacher said and then write a summary of each for tomorrow.

"Read the three cowboy stories," the teacher said, "and then write a summary of each for tomorrow."

1. He said the movie is about students who go to outer space by accident.

_____

2. We sang Big Rock Candy Mountain again.

_____

3. Bear, the Fire, and the Snow was her favorite poem by Shel Silverstein.

_____

4. We anticipate the weatherman said a foot of snow tomorrow.

_____

 **Write five sentences using quotations from people you have heard today. Share your sentences with a family member.**

Name _____ Date _____

Spelling: Digraphs *ch*, *sh*, *th*

Use with Student Book pages 184–185.

A. Write the word that has a consonant digraph. Then underline the digraph.

1. We ate lunch in the park.

_____

2. Should I meet you after class?

_____

3. My favorite subject is math. _____

4. I like crunchy peanut butter. _____

> **SPELLING TIP**
>
> The letter pairs *ch*, *sh*, and *th* all say one sound. These pairs can appear anywhere in a word.

B. Write *ch*, *sh*, or *th* to make a word. Then write the word.

5. ____ ____ o o s e   _____

6. f i ____ ____   _____

7. ____ ____ a n k   _____

8. r i ____ ____   _____

Use two of the answer words to write about a visit to a friend.

_____

_____

Home-School Connection

Write two words for each of the consonant digraphs. Show your words to a family member.

Writing: Write a Dialogue between Two Characters

Read the dialogue. Then read each question and circle the correct answer.

A Class Trip

(1) "I'm so glad our class visited the Children's Museum downtown on Monday, January 16th," said Maria. (2) What was your favorite part of the trip?"

(3) "I liked seeing the children's toys. (4) Some of them were more than one hundred and fifty years old," Henry answered.

(5) "I liked that exhibit too. (6) I didn't know kids played with dolls so long ago," said Maria. (7) "The doll faces were hand-painted!"

(8) Henry smiled. (9) "Let's go get a drink of water. (10) Can you imagine having no video games?" he asked.

(11) Maria laughed. (12) "No, I can't. (13) But is was amazing to go back in time for a few hours."

1. What is the BEST way to revise sentence 1?

   A "I'm so glad our class visited the Children's Museum," said Maria.

   B "I really loved the trip our class took to the Children's Museum downtown on Monday, January 16th, 2011," said Maria.

   C "We went to Children's Museum last week," said Maria.

   D No revision is needed.

2. Which sentence does NOT belong in this story?

   A Sentence 8

   B Sentence 9

   C Sentence 10

   D Sentence 11

3. What change, if any, should be made in sentence 13?

   A Change *amazing* to *amazed*

   B Change *few* to *many*

   C Change *is* to *it*

   D Make no change

Name _____ Date _____

Review

Use with Student Book pages 130–185.

A. Answer the questions after reading Unit 3. You can go back and reread to help find the answers.

1. Think of the sequence of events in *Why Mosquitoes Buzz in People's Ears*. Which sentence is NOT in the correct order? Circle the letter of the correct answer.

   A Monkey jumped to the highest tree.
   B One of Owl's eggs fell to the ground.
   C Lion told Mosquito he can never talk again.
   D Owl was sad and did not hoot.

2. Why did the animal council meet?

   _____

   _____

   _____

3. Circle the word that does NOT have a long vowel pair.

   wait   three   today   friend   toe   fruit

4. Circle the sentence that uses the verb *have* incorrectly.

   A The elves have an hour to make shoes.
   B Amelia has to get out of bed early.
   C Diego haves leather to make shoes.
   D Pixie and Lumkin have to leave soon.

5. Which question is NOT answered by the end of *John Henry and the Machine*? Circle the letter of the correct answer.

A What does John Henry love to do?

B Is John Henry stronger than a machine?

C How much did the stranger's machine cost?

D What does John Henry want to do when the contest is finished?

6. What was the stranger's mistake?

_____

7. According to the story, which can do more work, a machine or John Henry's sledgehammer?

_____

B. Read the dialogue from *The Shoemakers and the Elves*. Then answer questions 8 and 9.

Dialogue
Amelia: Look, Diego! Shoes! I must be dreaming!
Diego: Did you get up and work last night?
Amelia: No! I was going to ask you the same thing!

8. Draw a box around the word in the dialogue that has a vowel pair with the long *e* sound.

9. Circle the correct inference.

A Amelia is angry at Diego.

B Amelia likes the color of the shoes.

C Amelia thought Diego made the shoes.

D Amelia wants to thank the elves.

 Home-School Connection Tell a family member something new you learned from this unit.

110

Name _____   Date _____

Writing Workshop: Write a Story

Read the passage. Then read each question on the next page and circle the correct answer.

How Arrows Got Feathers

(1) A Caddo boy found a baby hawk. (2) The hawk could not fly. (3) The boy took the bird home. (4) He cared for it. (5) The hawk grew big and strong, or he did not want to leave the boy.

(6) One day, the boy was making arrows. (7) He shot the arrows into the air, but they all fell down.

(8) The hawk had an idea. (9) He dropped a his feather near the boy. (10) Then he dropped more and more feathers.

(11) Finally, the boy picked up the feathers, and he tied it to his arrow. (12) He shot the arrow, and it traveled straight and far. (13) This is how the Caddos started putting feathers on their arrows.

1. What change, if any, should be made in sentence 1?
   A Change *hawk* to *Hawk*
   B Change *found* to *founds*
   C Change *baby* to *baby's*
   D Make no change

2. What is the BEST way to combine sentences 3 and 4?
   A The boy took the bird home and cared for it.
   B The boy took and cared for the bird home.
   C The bird was carried home by the boy.
   D Took home the bird and he cared for it the boy.

3. What change, if any, should be made in sentence 5?
   A Change *grew* to *grown*
   B Change *want* to *wants*
   C Change *or* to *but*
   D Make no change

4. What is the BEST way to revise sentence 9?
   A He dropped a his feather near to the boy.
   B He dropped a feather near the boy.
   C He dropped near the boy a his feather.
   D No revision is needed.

5. What change, if any, should be made in sentence 11?
   A Change *his* to *the*
   B Change *picked* to *picks*
   C Change *it* to *them*
   D Make no change

Name _____ Date _____

Fluency

Use with Student Book page 193.

How fast are you? Use a clock. Read the text about mosquitoes. How long did it take you? Write your time in the chart. Read three times.

Why Mosquitoes Buzz in People's Ears tells the legend of Mosquito	11
and Turtle, and explains why people hear mosquitoes buzz in their	22
ears even today. Turtle did not want to listen to Mosquito's gossip,	34
and so she stuffed leaves in her ears. But then she couldn't hear	47
Snake, and this caused a big problem with Snake, Mouse, Rabbit,	58
Monkey, Owl, and Lion. One of Owl's eggs dropped to the ground.	70
She was so sad that she forgot to hoot the next morning to wake up	85
the sun. Because it was dark, Lion was unhappy. He asked the	97
animals questions and found out what happened. Everything had	106
happened because of Mosquito's gossip. Lion said Mosquito could	115
never talk again, only buzz.	120

My Times

Learning Checklist

Word Study and Phonics

☐ Long Vowel Pairs

☐ Vowel Pair: *ea*

☐ Synonyms and Antonyms

Strategies

☐ Identify Events in a Plot ☐ Infer and Predict

☐ Sequence of Events ☐ Identify Characters

☐ Make Inferences

Grammar

☐ Singular and Plural Nouns

☐ Possessives

☐ Quotations

Writing

☐ Retell a Familiar Story

☐ Write a Friendly Letter

☐ Write a Dialogue Between Two Characters

☐ Writing Workshop: Write a Story

Listening and Speaking

☐ Perform a Play

Name _____ Date _____

Test Preparation

Use with Student Book pages 194–195.

Read the selection. Then answer the questions.

(1) Once upon a time, Dog and Cat lived together. Dog said, "We need to share the work. I'll go find food, if you will take care of the house." Cat agreed, and Dog went to find food.

Cat jumped up to the window, where the warm sunshine poured in. "I think I'll take a little nap before I work. "

Day after day, it was the same. Cat slept while Dog worked. Every day, Dog came home and said, "What did you do all day, Cat? The house is a mess!" Cat just yawned.

(2) Then Dog got an idea. One day she told Cat she was going to work, but she hid under the sink instead. She watched Cat sleep all day. When Cat went to the sink to get a drink of water, Dog jumped out. "Yikes!" Cat screeched. Dog was furious and chased Cat around the room. That's how dogs started to chase cats.

1. What does Dog want Cat to do?
  A Share the work
  B Take a nap
  C Chase him around
  D Sit in the window

2. What is Cat like?
  F Hungry
  G Lazy
  H Busy
  J Angry

3. Where did Dog hide?
  A Under the sink
  B At work
  C Behind the house
  D Under the bed

4. Why did Dog chase Cat?
  F Cat ate all the food.
  G Cat did not keep her promise.
  H Cat hurt Dog's feelings.
  J Cat screeched at Dog.

Read the selection. Then answer the questions.

A thin wolf met a well-fed dog. The wolf said, "You always have food to eat. You look very strong. I am so hungry."

The dog said, "Come and work with me. Then you will always have food."

The wolf followed the dog. Then he saw something on the dog's neck. "What's that?" he asked the dog.

"Oh, it's nothing," said the dog. "The collar I wear at night rubs on my skin. Sometimes it hurts a little."

"A collar?" the wolf shouted. "Can't you always run free?"

"No, but it's OK," said the dog. When he heard that, the wolf ran into the forest. "Maybe I am hungry," he thought, "but I am free!"

1. What is the wolf's problem? He—

A wears a collar
B is free
C is well-fed
D is hungry

2. Why does the dog's neck hurt sometimes?

F He is well-fed.
G The collar rubs it.
H He can't run free.
L He runs in the forest.

3. The wolf runs into the forest because—

A he wants to get a collar
B he wants to find food
C he wants to be free
D he wants to be thin

4. How does the dog probably feel when the wolf runs into the forest?

F happy
G confused
H angry
J hungry

Name _____ Date _____

Key Words

Use with Student Book pages 202–203.

| vine |
| bean |
| celebration |
| gardener |
| roots |

A. Match each word with its definition. Write the letter of the correct answer.

1. vine _____ **A** a seed which you can eat

2. bean _____ **B** someone who grows vegetables, flowers, or plants

3. celebration _____ **C** part of a plant that takes in water and keeps it in place

4. gardener _____ **D** a plant that climbs

5. roots _____ **E** a party to mark a special occasion

B. Read each sentence. Write TRUE or FALSE.

6. A vine cannot grow up and around a tree. _____

7. Gardeners can grow vegetables and fruits. _____

8. The roots of a plant are underground. _____

9. A birthday celebration usually includes eating pie. _____

10. If you plant a bean, it can grow into a new plant. _____

Academic Words

Use with Student Book page 204.

affect
eliminate
outcome

**A. Choose the word that best completes each
sentence. Write the word.**

1. You can _____ your bad mood by exercising.

2. Too much water may _____ how well a plant grows.

3. If you don't study for a test, the _____ is usually not good.

**B. Choose the word that *best* matches the meaning of the
underlined words. Write the word.**

4. The gardener can <u>put an end to</u> animals eating her vegetables by
putting a fence around the garden. _____

5. Advertisements usually don't <u>have an influence</u> on me.

_____

6. The <u>end</u> of the football game was a tie. _____

C. Answer the questions.

7. What can your class do to help **eliminate** poverty?

_____

_____

8. When you are finished with school, what would you like the
outcome to be?

_____

_____

 **Use two vocabulary words to tell a family member what you
know about plants.**

Name _____ Date _____

Phonics: Soft and Hard *c*

Use with Student Book page 205.

> The letter *c* usually has the soft sound when it is followed by *e, i,* or *y,* as in *price*. Otherwise, the letter *c* usually has the hard sound as in *carry*.

A. Read each sentence. Underline the words that have the soft /s/ sound spelled *c*. Draw a box around the words that have the hard /k/ sound spelled *c*.

1. She can skate on ice.

2. The prince danced all night.

3. Who has the loudest voice in class?

4. Our cat was rescued by a fireman.

5. This sentence was written correctly.

B. Write each word in the correct column of the chart.

face   fact   cool   center   policy   candy

Soft *c* as in *mice*	Hard *c* as in *can*

Home-School Connection Think of two more examples of words with a soft *c* as in *mice* and two with a hard *c* as in *can*. Show your words to a family member.

Comprehension: The Trouble with Kudzu

Use with Student Book pages 206–209.

Answer the questions about the reading.

Recall

1. In the story "Jack and the Beanstalk," what did Jack plant?

_____

2. What is kudzu?

_____

3. When did the United States receive kudzu as a gift? Why?

_____

Comprehend

4. At first, why was kudzu a big success?

_____

_____

Analyze

5. Why is kudzu called a weed?

_____

_____

_____

Name _____ Date _____

Reader's Companion

Use with Student Book pages 206–209.

The Trouble with Kudzu

Kudzu is a native plant of China and Japan. That means it grew naturally in those countries. Kudzu was brought to the United States from Japan in 1876 as a gift for a special celebration. The United States was celebrating its first 100 years as a nation.

Soon, every gardener and farmer wanted to plant kudzu seeds. Gardeners grew kudzu because it looked pretty and smelled good. Farmers grew it to feed their animals.

At first kudzu was a big success! But it did not stop growing. It blocked sunlight that other plants needed. It killed trees and whole forests. Nothing was safe!

Genre

MARK the TEXT

Underline one sentence that tells you *The Trouble with Kudzu* is informational text.

Comprehension Check

List three things you know about kudzu.

1. _____

2. _____

3. _____

Use What You Know

What is the main idea of the second paragraph?

_____

Use the Strategy

Where did kudzu come from? What details in the passage helped you find the answer?

_____

_____

_____

Retell It!

Retell this passage as if you are a farmer. Describe what happened when you planted kudzu on your farm.

_____

_____

_____

_____

_____

_____

Reader's Response

What are two ways that kudzu became a problem?

_____

_____

_____

Summarize the passage for a family member.

Name _____ Date _____

Learning Strategies:
Main Idea and Details

Use with Student Book pages 210–211.

Read the newspaper article. Then answer the questions.

Corey Runs for Office

Corey James wants to be the next Student Council President! Every year, Lincoln Middle School has an election. Election Day will be on Tuesday, September 29. Susanna Clemons and Arturo Diaz are also running for the same office. "They are both good candidates," said Corey. "But I have more experience." Last year, Corey was the captain of the baseball team. He also was vice president of his class. "I know how to lead," said Corey. One of Corey's goals is to have a Holiday Fair. Many students like this idea. Maybe Corey will win the election.

1. What is the main idea of the paragraph?

_____

2. What details tell you that Corey may be a good candidate?

_____

_____

3. What other details do you know about the election?

_____

_____

Home-School Connection Find an article in the newspaper about something happening in your town today. How do the main idea and details help you understand the article? Share your ideas with a classmate.

123

Grammar: Comparatives

Use with Student Book pages 212–213.

Review the forms of **comparative adjectives**.

soft ➜ soft**er**	hot ➜ hott**er**	happy ➜ happ**ier**	beautiful ➜ **more** beautiful
good ➜ **better**	far ➜ **farther**	bad ➜ **worse**	fun ➜ **more** fun

Change each adjective to the correct comparative and rewrite the sentence.

Example: The beans tasted (good) _____ than the last time we had them.

The beans tasted <u>better</u> than the last time we had them.

1. The vine climbed the (tall) _____ tree in the forest.

_____

2. This garden is (green) _____ than it was last year.

_____

3. She was (careful) _____ with her homework after seeing her report card.

_____

4. He said his grandfather's birthday party was (crazy) _____ than his cousin's.

_____

5. The water is (deep) _____ than it was before the rain.

_____

 Write five sentences using comparatives to describe which foods you like and dislike. Share your sentences with a family member.

Name _____ Date _____

Spelling: /g/ and /j/ Sounds Spelled *g*

Use with Student Book pages 214–215.

**Write the word that matches each clue.
Then circle what sound the letter *g*
makes in each word.**

game	giraffe
great	gold
Georgia	

**SPELLING
TIP**

The letter *g* stands for
two sounds: /g/ and /j/.
Many words beginning
with *g* have the /g/
sound. If the vowels *i* or
e follow *g*, the sound
may be /j/.

1. very good _____ /g/ sound /j/ sound

2. shiny yellow _____ /g/ sound /j/ sound

3. animal with a long neck _____ /g/ sound /j/ sound

4. something you play _____ /g/ sound /j/ sound

5. state in the South _____ /g/ sound /j/ sound

Use three of the spelling words in sentences.

_____

_____

_____

_____

**Home-School
Connection**   Look through the *G*s in the dictionary. Find two words each that begin with
the /g/ and /j/ sounds spelled *g*. Show your words to a family member.

125

Writing: Write a Persuasive Business Letter

Read the letter. Then read each question and circle the correct answer.

(1) Dear Ms. Hughes,

(2) The students at Webster School need art supplies for our classes. (3) Without these supplies, our art classes will be cancelled.

(4) These classes are fun. (5) Also, art skills are more important today than ever before. (6) These skills will help us find better jobs in the future. (7) Research shows that older workers with these skills can design more interesting ads, signs, commercials, and web sites. (8) It's important to have more art classes, not fewer ones.

(9) We hope that you will donate the art supplies that our school needs to continue these classes.

(10) Please, please, we beg you, help us out. (11) Thank you for your time.

(12) Sincerely,

(13) Tony Liu

1. What change, if any, should be made in sentence 1?

   A Change *Dear* to *Deer*

   B Change *Ms. Hughes* to *Kim Hughes*

   C Change the comma to a colon

   D Make no change

2. What change, if any, should be made in sentence 7?

   A Add the word *someday*

   B Delete the word *older*

   C Change *skills* to *computer skills*

   D Change *more* to *most*

3. Which sentence does NOT belong in this letter?

   A Sentence 5

   B Sentence 7

   C Sentence 8

   D Sentence 10

Name _____ Date _____

Key Words

Use with Student Book pages 216–217.

flatter
praise
advice
guzzled
scampered
scam

A. Choose the word that *best* completes each sentence. Write the word.

1. If you want to _____ someone, just tell them something you really like about them.

2. The dog _____ under the bed every time there was thunderstorm.

3. They should _____ the firemen for rescuing their cat from the tree.

4. He liked to ask the _____ of his grandparents because they were very wise.

5. After the race she _____ ice water to cool herself off.

B. Write the correct word for each sentence.

6. The team (guzzled/scampered) water after the game.
_____

7. She will (flatter/praise) you and tell you how good you look when she wants to borrow something. _____

8. My mom always gives me good (praise/advice) when I am not sure what to do. _____

9. I can never tell if he's being honest or just polite when he (guzzles/praises) my cooking. _____

10. He (scampered/guzzled) up the mountain to get away from the bear. _____

Academic Words

Use with Student Book page 218.

> evaluate
> resourceful
> scheme

A. Choose the word that best completes each sentence. Write the word.

1. I liked that movie because you didn't know the thief's _____ for stealing the jewels.

2. If you _____ the advertisement carefully you can usually tell it is not true.

3. On rainy days you need to be _____ to avoid being bored.

B. Choose the word that *best* matches the meaning of the underlined words. Write the word.

4. Her projects always look great because she's so <u>creative</u>. _____

5. It's not simple to <u>judge</u> which plan is better. _____

6. We missed one detail when we planned our <u>strategy</u>. _____

C. Answer the questions.

7. How do you **evaluate** if an advertisement is honest?

_____

_____

8. How can you be **resourceful** in finding out the answer to a difficult homework problem?

_____

_____

Use a thesaurus to find synonyms for three of the vocabulary words.

Name _____ Date _____

Word Study: Thesaurus
Use with Student Book page 219.

> A **dictionary** tells the meaning of a word.
> A **thesaurus** lists synonyms or words with similar meanings.

Read the sentence and the definition for each underlined word. Then write the synonym that is closest in meaning to the underlined word.

1. My answer to the last question was <u>wrong</u>. _____

    wrong *adjective* / not correct: *a wrong turn*

    SYNONYMS: **incorrect** / inaccurate, faulty: *an incorrect conclusion*

                bad / below an accepted level: *bad quality*

2. The <u>last</u> bus left at midnight. _____

    last *adjective* / final in a series: *the last stop*

    SYNONYMS: **final** / the end position: *the final station*

                previous / most recent: *previous job*

3. Will you <u>correct</u> this mistake? _____

    correct *verb* / to remove the errors from: *correct the spelling mistakes*

    SYNONYMS: **improve** / to make better: *improve your work habits*

                fix / to make right: *fix a broken bike*

Find three synonyms for the word *good*. Look up each word in the dictionary and use it in a sentence. Show your sentences to a family member.

129

Comprehension:
The Fox and the Crow/The Fox and the Goat

Use with Student Book pages 220–223.

Answer the questions about the reading.

Recall

1. What did Ms. Crow have that Mr. Fox wanted?

_____

2. What did Mr. Fox say about Ms. Crow's feathers and eyes?

_____

3. How did Mr. Fox get out of the well?

_____

Comprehend

4. How did Mr. Fox fool Ms. Crow and Mr. Goat?

_____

_____

Analyze

5. Evaluate the actions of Mr. Fox. Do you think what he did was wrong?

_____

_____

_____

Name _____ Date _____

Reader's Companion

Use with Student Book pages 220–223.

The Fox and the Crow

Just then, Mr. Fox heard wings flapping overhead, and he looked up to see a crow with a large piece of cheese in its beak. The crow landed in a tree nearby and Mr. Fox thought to himself, *That cheese looks very tasty. I must find a way to get it.* Being a clever fellow, he soon came up with an idea.

The Fox and the Goat

Mr. Fox fell into a well one day and could not find a way to get out. But just as he was about to give up hope, Mr. Goat looked over the edge of the well.

"Oh, I am so thirsty, Fox," he said. "Is the water good? And by the way, what are you doing in the well?"

Right away, Mr. Fox saw his chance to escape, so he said, "I am enjoying the water, of course! You should jump in and have a drink."

Use What You Know

List three things you know about fables.

1. _____

2. _____

3. _____

Learning Strategy

MARK the TEXT

Circle one thing that is the same about the fox in both passages.

Comprehension Check

Who is the fox trying to help in the stories? Underline the information that tells you this.

MARK the TEXT

Use the Strategy

Compare the fox in both passages. How is he similar? Then contrast the crow and the goat. How are they different?

_____

_____

_____

Retell It!

Retell this passage as if you were the crow or the goat talking about what happened.

_____

_____

_____

_____

_____

Reader's Response

Is the fox good or bad in these stories? Why?

_____

_____

_____

Summarize the passage for a family member.

Name _____ Date _____

Learning Strategies:
Compare and Contrast

Use with Student Book pages 224–225.

A. Compare and contrast the items. List two ways they are alike. Then list two ways they are different.

1. a house and an apartment building

alike _____

different _____

2. a cookie and a pie

alike _____

different _____

B. Read the travel article. Compare and contrast the two cities.

Two Cities

Chicago and London are big cities. Chicago is in the middle of the United States. It is on the shore of Lake Michigan. London is in England. The Thames River goes through London. There are parks and paths in both cities. But unlike London, Chicago also has beaches on the lake.

_____

_____

_____

_____

Think of two cities you want to visit. Write two sentences that compare the cities. Then write two sentences that contrast the cities. Show your sentences to a family member.

Grammar: Superlatives

Use with Student Book pages 226–227.

Review the forms of **superlative adjectives**.

| **small** cake → small**est** cake | expensive gift → **most** expensive gift |

Change each adjective to a superlative. Add *-est* or *most*. Remember to add *the*. Write the sentences.

Example: He always gives me (high) praise of anyone.

He always gives me the highest praise of anyone.

1. It was (bad) snowstorm in twenty years.

_____

2. I went to the circus and saw (crazy) clown I've ever seen.

_____

3. It was not (comfortable) bed I had slept in.

_____

4. She has (blue) eyes of everyone in her family.

_____

5. The company makes (cheap) toys.

_____

Write five sentences using superlatives. Share your sentences with a family member.

Name _____ Date _____

Spelling: Use a Dictionary

Use with Student Book pages 228–229.

Use the dictionary definitions to answer the questions.

> **cool** /kool/
>
> 1. **adjective** A little bit cold. *The weather will be cool tonight.*
>
> 2. **verb** To lower the temperature of something. *We can't eat the cookies until they cool.*
>
> 3. **adjective** Unfriendly and distant. *Chico gave me a cool look when he heard my news.*

SPELLING TIP

How can you find a word in the dictionary if you don't know how to spell it? Say the word. What is the first sound? Write that letter. Then say the word again, listen to the next sound, and write it down. Soon, you will have enough letters to help you find the word.

1. What does /kool/ tell you? _____

2. How many definitions are given for *cool* when it is used as an adjective? _____

3. Write the definition of *cool* as a word that refers to temperature.

_____

 Write a short magazine article about an art exhibit. Use two forms of the word *show* in your writing.

_____

_____

_____

Home-School Connection

Look up the dictionary definitions for the word *research*. Explain how the word was used in the reading. Use two forms of the word in sentences. Share your sentences with a family member.

Writing: Write an Advertisement

Read the advertisement. Then read each question and circle the correct answer.

(1) The "Pack Light" is today's newest backpack!

(2) • It's the most lightweight backpack sold!

(3) • It holds books and supplies in five different compartments!

(4) • Its easy to pack and unpack!

(5) • Its zippers are the strongest!

(6) • More than 10,000 "Pack Lights" sold, so that proves this is a top-of-the-line pack!

(7) Carrying a "Pack Light" makes a different. (8) Be the coolest kid in class. (9) Buy one today.

1. What change, if any, should be made in sentence 3?
   A Change *five* to *5*
   B Change *supplies* to *supplys*
   C Change *different* to *difference*
   D Make no change

2. What change, if any, should be made in sentence 4?
   A Change *and* to *or*
   B Change *Its* to *It's*
   C Change the exclamation point to a period
   D Make no change

3. What change, if any, should be made in sentence 7?
   A Add a comma after *Light*
   B Change *makes* to *make*
   C Change *different* to *difference*
   D Make no change

Name _____ Date _____

Key Words

Use with Student Book pages 230–231.

communities
preserve
architects
original
concerned
purpose

A. Choose the word that *best* completes each sentence. Write the word.

1. He was _____ about his friend because she had been sick for a week.

2. Luckily I only threw out the copy and not the _____.

3. The carpenters followed the plans drawn by the _____.

4. _____ from every town in the state were represented at the state fair.

5. She took a picture of the pretty flowers so she could _____ the memory of them.

6. She understood the _____ of the homework when she finished it.

B. Unscramble the words. Then write a definition for the word.

7. t i s c r a t c h e _____

_____

8. v e e r e r s p _____

_____

9. p e r s o u p _____

_____

Academic Words

Use with Student Book page 232.

objective
restore
site

A. Choose the word that best completes each sentence. Write the word.

1. His hobby was to _____ old furniture to its original condition.

2. An architect carefully chooses the _____ for the building.

3. The most important _____ for the skater was not to fall.

B. Choose the word that *best* matches the meaning of the underlined words. Write the word.

4. The <u>purpose</u> of the meeting was to decide who had the best plan.

   _____

5. The community did not like the <u>location</u> for the new movie theater.

   _____

6. The choice was between <u>repairing</u> the car and buying a new one.

   _____

C. Answer the questions.

7. Why might you **restore** a book rather than buy a new one?

   _____

   _____

8. Are there any **sites** of events from history you would like to visit?

   _____

   _____

Think of a second answer for each of the questions. Share your answers with a family member.

Name _____ Date _____

Phonics: Digraph *ow*

Use with Student Book page 233.

> The **digraph *ow*** can have the long *o* sound you
> hear in *grow* or the vowel sound you hear in *how*.

**A. Read each sentence. Underline the words with *ow* that have a
long *o* sound. Draw a box around the words with *ow* that have
the vowel sound as in the word *how*.**

1. The clown was in the show.

2. Do you know what town she lives in?

3. Plow trucks come out when it snows.

4. I like red and yellow flowers the best!

5. Will you throw the ball to me now?

B. Write each word in the correct column of the chart.

allow	below	now	slow	throw	towel

ow spells the long *o* sound as in *grow*	*ow* spells the vowel sound as in *how*

Home-School Connection Think of three more examples of *ow* words for each vowel sound.
Show your words to a family member.

Comprehension: New Life for Old Buildings

Use with Student Book pages 234–237.

Answer the questions about the reading.

Recall

1. How are buildings like people?

_____

2. Who worked in the Old State Capitol in Springfield, Illinois?

_____

3. What materials were used to make many old buildings?

_____

Comprehend

4. Why would vacant buildings be a problem in urban and rural areas?

_____

_____

Analyze

5. How does restoring old buildings help a community?

_____

_____

_____

Name _____   Date _____

Reader's Companion

Use with Student Book pages 234–237.

New Life for Old Buildings

You might be surprised to know that buildings are like people in some ways. Like people, they have a story to tell. Like each person, each building has a past.

Now communities are trying to preserve their old buildings. Factories, train stations, churches, and schools are getting new lives!

Have you ever visited an old building and wondered about its history? Did you try to picture who lived or worked there? Imagine visiting an art gallery that was once a jail. Now it holds art instead of prisoners.

Not long ago, people tore down old buildings that were no longer suitable for their original purposes. Usually, they replaced old buildings with new ones. Sometimes they just left empty lots. When these buildings came down, people lost important links to the past.

Genre

Underline one sentence that tells you *New Life for Old Buildings* is informational text.

Reading Strategy

Circle one sentence that gives an example of a cause and its effect.

Comprehension Check

List kinds of buildings that are being reused for a different purpose.

1. _____

2. _____

3. _____

Use the Strategy

What happens when people tear down an old building? To find the answer, look for cause and effect in the first paragraph.

_____

_____

_____

Retell It!

Retell this passage as if you are the mayor of a town. Tell why you want people to preserve old buildings.

_____

_____

_____

_____

_____

Reader's Response

What old building in your community do you think should be salvaged? How would you reuse the building?

_____

_____

_____

Copyright © by Pearson Education, Inc.

Summarize the passage for a family member.

Name _____ Date _____

Learning Strategies: Cause and Effect

Use with Student Book pages 238–239.

A. Match each cause with its effect. Write the letter of the correct answer.

Cause	Effect
1. We lost power after a big storm.	**A** We couldn't use the computer.
2. My dad got a new job.	**B** She did well on the test.
3. Erin studied every night.	**C** A police officer had to direct traffic.
4. A traffic light broke.	**D** We moved to another city.

B. Read the passage. Then complete the chart.

Our New House

Mom and Dad saved money for a long time. Finally they could buy a new house. The house was very old. It needed many repairs. There was a lot of work to be done, so everybody had to help. My sister and I painted the kitchen. My brothers planted trees. Now our yard looks like a forest!

Cause	Effect
Mom and Dad saved money.	
	The house needed repairs.
My brothers planted trees.	

Pretend it snowed last night. Write three sentences that explain the snow storm's effect. Show your sentences to a family member.

Grammar: Adverbs of Frequency and Intensity

Use with Student Book pages 240–241.

Review the forms of **adverbs of frequency and intensity.**

He is **always** late.   He **always comes** to class late.   Today he is **very late.**

A. **Fill in the blanks with the adverb of frequency that works** *best* **in the sentence. Use the words in the box.**

always	often	sometimes	rarely	never

Example: She <u>never</u> gives surprise quizzes because she thinks they are unfair.

1. They _____ have dinner with their grandparents because they live so close.

2. The dentist reminds him to _____ brush his teeth before going to bed.

3. We almost _____ are bored because there is so much to do in our neighborhood.

B. **Fill in the blanks with the adverb of intensity that works** *best* **in the sentence. Use the words in the box.**

almost	just	too	very	hardly

Example: We were _____ home when the care broke down.
We were <u>almost</u> home when the care broke down.

4. He said, "You can never have _____ many friends."

5. The temperature outside was _____ cold enough that he wore a jacket.

6. You must study a _____ long time to master the game of chess.

Write five sentences about what you regularly do and don't do on the weekends using adverbs of frequency and intensity. Share your sentences with a family member.

144

Copyright © by Pearson Education, Inc.

Name _____ Date _____

Spelling: The /f/ Sound Spelled *ph*

Use with Student Book pages 242–243.

alphabet	dolphin	elephant
Joseph	nephew	paragraphs

SPELLING TIP

Sometimes the /f/ sound is not spelled with the letter *f*. The letters *ph* also can spell /f/.

Write each word in the correct category.

Animals	
People	
Things You Learn about in English Class	

Choose one of the categories. Write two sentences using the words from that category.

_____

_____

_____

_____

Write two more words with the /f/ sound spelled *ph*. Show your words to a family member.

145

Writing: Write a Persuasive Brochure

Read the brochure. Then read each question and circle the correct answer.

(1) Come to the opening of the Morris Park Kennel. (2) This modern dog run has separate dog runs for large and small dogs. (3) We want our dogs to be healthy. (4) The dog run will be cleaned every day. (5) We want our dogs to be happy. (6) All dogs must be well behaved. (7) We want our neighbors to be happy. (8) If dogs bark too loudly, they will have to leave. (9) Please mark the opening of the new dog run on your calendar! (10) Friday, September 10 at 9 A.M. (11) Morris Park Kennel (12) 205 Morris Avenue (13) We will be very pleased to welcome you and your dog! (14) There will be free dog treats!

1. What is the BEST way to revise sentence 2?

 A This modern dog run has separate dog runs for large dogs and small dogs.

 B This modern dog kennel has separate runs for large and small dogs.

 C This modern dog run has separate dog runs for all different sizes and kinds of dogs.

 D No revision is needed.

2. What is the BEST way to revise sentences 3 and 4?

 A We want our dogs to be healthy, however, the dog run will be cleaned every day.

 B For very healthy dogs, the dog runs will be cleaned every day.

 C Because we want healthy dogs, the dog runs will be cleaned every day.

 D No revision is needed.

3. What is the BEST way to revise sentences 5 and 6?

 A We want our dogs to be happy, therefore all dogs must be well behaved.

 B Only the happiest dogs will be allowed to stay.

 C Dogs that misbehave will have to leave.

 D No revision is needed.

Name _____ Date _____

Review

Use with Student Book pages 196–243.

**Answer the questions after reading Unit 4. You can
go back and reread to help find the answers.**

1. Which question is not answered by the end of *New Life for Old
Buildings*? Circle the letter of the correct answer.

   A Why do some people want to save old buildings?

   B Which architect saved an old schoolhouse?

   C Can people reuse old buildings?

   D Are people finding creative ways to use old buildings?

2. Write a sentence telling why an old building can be
a link to our past.

_____

_____

3. Underline the sentence that does not have a frequency adverb in it.
Circle the letter of the correct answer.

   A They are often strong and beautiful.

   B Old buildings were usually made with stone and brick.

   C The number of people using the church grew too large.

   D After a building is destroyed, we can never see it again.

4. Write the frequency adverbs that appear in the three other
sentences.

_____

5. Circle the word that has the hard *c* sound.

   campaign   change   policy   dance

Read this passage from *The Trouble with Kudzu*. Then answer questions 6 and 7.

> Over the years, people have learned to use every part of the kudzu plant. Cooks and artists use it to make jelly, paper, clothes, baskets, and chairs. This weed might be useful after all.

6. Identify the genre of the passage. Circle the letter of the correct answer.

A friendly letter   **B** informational text   **C** how-to poster

7. What is the main idea of the paragraph? _____

Read this passage from *The Fox and the Crow*. Then answer questions 8 and 9.

> He continued, "Your voice must be even more beautiful than the lovely picture you make sitting in that tree. I am sure if I could hear you sing, I would call you the Queen of Birds!" Ms. Crow opened her beak to caw. Out fell the cheese, and Mr. Fox snapped it up.

8. When the fox says this to the crow, he is _____ her.

A praising   **B** guzzling   **C** flattering   **D** scampering

9. Which sentence *best* completes the Cause and Effect Chart?

Cause	Effect
	The Fox gets the crow's cheese.

A The fox asks the crow to sing.
B The fox says the crow is beautiful.
C The fox gave the crow some advice.
D The fox said the crow is lovely.

Tell a family member something new you learned from this unit.

Name _____ Date _____

Writing Workshop: Write a Review

Read the passage. Then read each question on the next page and circle the correct answer.

My Book Review

(1) I read a great book called *2030: A Day in the Life of Tomorrow's Kids* by Amy Zuckerman and Jim Daly. (2) This book talks about a day in the life of some students in 2030. (3) The kids does regular things, like getting up and going to school, but many new inventions make their day different.

(4) I like this book because it is not really science fiction. (5) You can find it in a bookstore or a library. (6) The authors are guessing about life 2030. (7) They asked many scientists for advice on the inventions in the book.

(8) If you like Science, or if you like science fiction, you will like this book. (9) It is exciting to see the future.

1. What is the BEST way to revise sentence 2?

    A This book talks about the life in a day some students in 2030.

    B About a day in the life this book talks of some students in 2030.

    C One day this book talks about the life of some students in 2030.

    D No revision is needed.

2. What change, if any, should be made in sentence 3?

    A Change *make* to *makes*

    B Change *inventions* to *invention*

    C Change *does* to *do*

    D Make no change

3. What change, if any, should be made in sentence 6?

    A Change *2030* to *in 2030*

    B Change *2030* to *at 2030*

    C Change *2030* to *on* 2030

    D Make no change

4. What change, if any, should be made in sentence 8?

    A Change *this* to *these*

    B Change *Science* to *science*

    C Change *or* to *but*

    D Make no change

5. Which sentence does NOT belong in this story?

    A Sentence 2

    B Sentence 4

    C Sentence 5

    D Sentence 8

Name _____ Date _____

Fluency

Use with Student Book page 251.

How fast are you? Use a clock. Read the text about *New Life for Old Buildings*. How long did it take you? Write your time in the chart. Read three times.

New Life for Old Buildings tells why tearing down old buildings	11
and leaving empty lots is a big problem. Like a person, each old	24
building has a past history. When people tear down a building,	35
they lose an important reminder of the past.	43
Now communities are trying to preserve old buildings. They use	53
these old buildings for a new purpose. For example, some mansions	64
have become museums. Some schools have become apartment	72
buildings, and some railroad stations have become shopping	80
centers. People in Littleton, Colorado, built a train station in 1888.	91
It was empty for years. Then it became the Depot Art Center and	104
Gallery. Old buildings that are preserved provide an example of	114
the past.	116

My Times

Learning Checklist

Word Study and Phonics

☐ Soft and Hard *c*

☐ Thesaurus

☐ Digraph: *ow*

Strategies

☐ Main Idea and Details

☐ Compare and Contrast

☐ Identify Cause and Effect

Grammar

☐ Comparatives

☐ Superlatives

☐ Adverbs of Frequency and Intensity

Writing

☐ Write a Persuasive Business Letter

☐ Write an Advertisement

☐ Write a Persuasive Brochure

☐ Writing Workshop: Write a Review

Listening and Speaking

☐ Give a Speech

Name _____ Date _____

Test Preparation

Use with Student Book pages 252–253.

Read the selection. Look for any corrections and improvements that may be needed, then answer the questions.

(1) At tonight's town meeting, the City Council will announce its decision to make skateboarding on the sidewalk against the law. (2) Too many skateboarders have run into people and cars. (3) These accidents are making people verry angry. (4) But responsible skateboarders are angry, too. (5) Parents of skateboarders may be angryier than the kids. (6) They will have to pay fines if their kids are caught skateboarding on the sidewalk. (7) Mr. Ikeda has offered to give the town a plot of land to build a skateboard park. (8) It's a great offer, but we need money to build it. (9) Come to the town meeting, and shar your ideas!

1. What change, if any, should be made in sentence 3?

  A Change *accidents* to **accident**

  B Change *are* to **is**

  C Change *These* to **This**

  D Change *verry* to **very**

2. Which change, if any, is needed in sentence 5?

  F Change *Parents* to **Parents'**

  G Change *are* to **is**

  H Change *angryier* to **angrier**

  J Make no change

3. What change, if any, should be made in sentence 8?

  A Change *money* to **mony**

  B Change *It's* to **Its**

  C Delete **it**

  D Make no change

4. What change, if any, should be made in sentence 9?

  F Change *town* to **towns**

  G Change *shar* to **share**

  H Delete **meeting**

  J Make no change

Read the selection. Look for any corrections and improvements that may be needed, then answer the questions.

(1) Plainfield schools are thinking about changing the starting time of the skool day. (2) Now school starts at 7:45 A.M. (3) They want to move the starting time to 9:15 A.M. (4) Why should we start our school day later? (5) Some Scientists say that students need more sleep. (6) Many students at plainfield schools wake up at 6:00 A.M. (7) Because of this, they are tire at school. If the starting time is 9:15 A.M., students can sleep more. (8) Students who sleep more can do a better job. (9) Please call the Plainfield school office. (10) Tell them you agree with their plan.

1. What change, if any, should be made in sentence 1?
  A Change *changing* to changeing
  B Change *skool* to school
  C Change *thinking* to think
  D Make no change.

2. Which change, if any, is needed in sentence 5?
  F Change *need* to needing
  G Change *students* to student
  H Change *Scientists* to scientists
  J Make no change

3. What change, if any, should be made in sentence 6?
  A Change *plainfield* to **Plainfield**
  B Change *wake* to **woke**
  C Delete **at**
  D Make no change

4. What change, if any, should be made in sentence 7?
  F Delete **more**
  G Change *this,* to **this**
  H Change *tire* to **tired**
  J Make no change

Name _____ Date _____

Key Words

Use with Student Book pages 260–261.

native
extreme
architecture
underground
mining
efficient

**A. Match each word with its definition.
Write the letter of the correct answer.**

1. native _____   **A** taking things like gold from below the ground

2. underground _____   **B** good at not wasting time

3. mining _____   **C** the look of a building

4. efficient _____   **D** not normal or usual

5. architecture _____   **E** from a particular place

6. extreme _____   **F** below the surface of the earth

B. Choose the word that *best* completes each sentence. Write the word.

7. The workers dug a tunnel deep

_____.

8. Polar bears can live in _____ cold.

9. Workers look for gold when _____.

10. What animals are _____ to your state?

11. I never waste time because I am _____!

12. Beautiful well-made buildings show why _____ is important.

Academic Words

Use with Student Book page 262.

> adapt
> environment
> located

A. Match each word with its definition. Write the letter of the correct answer.

1. adapt   _____   **A**   be in a particular place

2. environment   _____   **B**   adjust to new conditions

3. located   _____   **C**   surroundings

B. Choose the word that best completes each sentence. Write the word.

4. We can _____ to the rainy weather by moving the party to the garage.

5. They had all the resources they needed to create the best learning _____.

6. The music room is _____ in the basement.

C. Answer the questions.

7. If you had to go to a new school, how would you **adapt**?

  _____

  _____

8. Describe the **environment** around your house.

  _____

  _____

Copyright © by Pearson Education, Inc.

 Home-School Connection   Define three academic words in your own words. Show your definitions to a family member.

Name _____ Date _____

Word Study: Homophones

Use with Student Book page 263.

> **Homophones** are words that sound the same but have different spellings and meanings.

Read each homophone pair. Then choose the word that best completes each sentence.

1. | ate, eight | I _____ breakfast with my dad.

My brother is _____ years old.

2. | hear, here | Do you live _____ or over there?

Did you _____ that noise?

3. | sail, sale | She bought a shirt at the _____.

We _____ our boat on the lake.

4. | flour, flower | My baker needs _____ to make bread.

Only one _____ bloomed in the garden.

5. | knew, new | There is a _____ student in class.

Suzanne _____ every answer on the test.

6. | sea, see | They couldn't _____ anything in the dark.

We traveled by boat across the _____.

Use each of these words in sentences: *to, two, too.* Show your sentences to a family member.

157

Comprehension: The Underground City

Use with Student Book pages 264–267.

Answer the questions about the reading.

Recall

1. How many people live in Coober Pedy, Australia?

_____

2. Why do many of the people of Coober Pedy live in underground houses?

_____

3. What are native to Coober Pedy?

_____

Comprehend

4. How did the underground homes in Coober Pedy begin?

_____

_____

Analyze

5. Why do you think the people of Coober Pedy are able to adapt to the extreme heat?

_____

_____

_____

Name _____   Date _____

Reader's Companion

Use with Student Book pages 264–267.

The Underground City

About 3,500 people live in Coober Pedy, Australia. From the street, you might see only dirt and some trees. But under the ground, there are homes! More than half of the people in the town live in underground houses. These are regular houses that look a lot like yours!

The summer heat in Coober Pedy is extreme. But the underground homes are efficient. They stay cool during the hot months. That means people don't spend money on air conditioning. In the winter, the homes stay warm and that means people pay less for heat.

Use What You Know

List three things you know about Coober Pedy, Australia.

1. _____

2. _____

3. _____

Reading Strategy

Underline one fact from the passage. Circle one opinion from the passage.

Comprehension Check

Put a line through one sentence that explains how Coober Pedy's underground homes are efficient.

Use the Strategy

Find one fact in the first paragraph of the passage. Explain why it is a fact and not an opinion.

_____

_____

_____

Retell It!

Retell this passage as if you want a friend to move to Coober Pedy, Australia.

_____

_____

_____

_____

_____

Reader's Response

Would you like to live in an underground house? Why or why not?

_____

_____

_____

Summarize the passage for a family member.

160

Name _____ Date _____

Learning Strategies: Fact and Opinion

Use with Student Book pages 268–269.

Read each sentence. Write F for fact or O for opinion.

1. Living underground is fun! _____

2. I think everyone in class is nice. _____

3. Mining is dangerous work. _____

4. Most people want to live near the ocean. _____

5. Deserts have extreme weather. _____

6. Everyone in class took the test. _____

7. Summer weather is terrible! _____

8. Kids like going to school every day. _____

9. Many people live near oceans and lakes. _____

10. Some homes are built of wood and stone. _____

Home-School Connection

Imagine you live underground. Write one fact and one opinion about living underground. Show your fact and opinion to a family member.

161

Grammar: Capitalizing Proper Nouns

Use with Student Book pages 270–271.

Days of the week and months	Sunday, Monday / March, April
Historical events and documents	Declaration of Independence
Titles of books, stories, and essays	The Wind in the Willows
Languages, races, and nationalities	English, Hispanic, Canadian

Rewrite each sentence using correct capitalization.

Example: on saturday the miranda family went to the mall.

<u>On Saturday the Miranda family went to the mall.</u>

1. meet me at turner playground near the kennedy school.

_____

2. pedro's english skills have really improved since the fall.

_____

3. do you think your mom will let you go to philip's party at the end of august?

_____

4. the egyptian pharoahs, like tutankhamun, were buried in the pyramids.

_____

5. we are taking a vacation to arizona to see the grand canyon this summer.

_____

Write five sentences, one for each weekday (Monday through Friday), about what you did last week. Include the names of specific people and places in your sentences. Share your sentences with a family member.

Name _____ Date _____

Spelling: /s/ Sound Spelled c

Use with Student Book pages 272–273.

Fill in each blank with a letter to solve the clue.

> **SPELLING TIP**
>
> When the letter c makes the s sound, e, i, or y always follows the c.

1. frozen water _____ c e

2. large town c i _____ _____

3. round shape c i _____ _____ _____ _____

4. two wheels that you can ride _____ _____ c y _____ _____ _____

5. cats chase them _____ _____ c e

6. the middle c e _____ _____ _____ _____

7. coin worth one c e _____ _____

8. good or friendly _____ _____ c e

9. your eyes and mouth are on it _____ _____ c e

10. not plain _____ _____ _____ c y

 Write sentences using two of the answer words.

_____

_____

_____

_____

 Write four more words that have the /s/ sound spelled c. Two of the words should begin with the /s/ sound; two of the words should have the /s/ sound. Show your words to a family member.

Writing: Write to Classify

Read the selection. Then read each question and circle the correct answer.

(1) While most birds fly, some birds can't fly. (2) Flying birds have longer wings but fewer feathers. (3) An owl is a flying bird that eats meat and hunts at night. (4) An ostrich is a fast-running, flightless bird that lives in Africa. (5) Owls are found in north America and rain forests in south America.

(6) Flightless birds first developed on islands. (7) There they had few enemies to fly away from. (8) These birds have shortest wings. (9) They have more feathers all over their bodies. (10) These giants are the largest and heaviest of all birds.

1. What change, if any, should be made in sentence 5?
   A Change *are found* to *were found*
   B Change *rain forests* to *Rain Forests*
   C Change *north* and south to *North and South*
   D Make no change

2. Which sentence is out of order?
   A Sentence 4
   B Sentence 5
   C Sentence 6
   D Sentence 9

3. Where should the sentence you chose in question 2 be put?
   A Before sentence 3
   B After sentence 8
   C Before sentence 7
   D After sentence 9

4. What change, if any, should be made in sentence 8?
   A Change *shortest* to *short*
   B Change *These* to *Those*
   C Change *have* to *has*
   D Make no change

Name _____ Date _____

Key Words

Use with Student Book pages 274–275.

prairie
sod
climate
harsh
record

A. Choose the word that *best* matches the meaning of the underlined words. Write the word.

1. The <u>usual weather</u> is hot and rainy.

   _____

2. Snow and ice make winters seem <u>extreme</u>. _____

3. Cows spend their days on the <u>very large grasslands</u>.

   _____

4. The <u>thick layer of grass</u> feels soft under our feet. _____

5. The girls kept a <u>written history</u> of their experiences.

   _____

B. Choose the word that *best* completes each sentence. Write the word.

6. Our front yard is covered with thick _____.

7. A report card is a _____ of your grades.

8. Wild animals lived on the _____.

9. It snows a lot in places where the _____ is cold.

10. When the weather is _____, I play indoors.

Academic Words

Use with Student Book page 276.

A. **Choose the word that *best* completes each sentence. Write the word.**

1. Every summer they _____ in a house by the beach.

2. We use a secret code when we _____ with one another.

3. _____ I didn't know how to ride a bicycle. Now I ride every day.

B. **Choose the word that *best* matches the meaning of the underlined words. Write the word.**

4. In the past I liked kickball, but now I play soccer. _____

5. We plan to stay with my cousins this summer. _____.

6. My best friend and I can communicate using our computers.

_____

C. **Answer the questions.**

7. Describe the house where you **reside**.

_____

_____

8. Who would you like to **correspond** with?

_____

_____

Use the vocabulary words to tell about life on the prairie.

Name _____ Date _____

Phonics: Y as a Vowel

Use with Student Book page 277.

> The letter **y** sometimes acts as a vowel.
> - **The letter y usually has the long i sound when it comes after a consonant at the end of a one-syllable word.**
> - **The letter y usually has the long e sound when it comes after a consonant at the end of a word with more than one syllable.**

Read each sentence. Underline the word that has the long e or long i sound spelled y. Then circle the correct sound. The first one is done for you.

1. We are moving to the <u>city</u>.   (long e)   long i

2. You should try to visit us.   long e   long i

3. The baby will have a big room.   long e   long i

4. My new room has two closets.   long e   long i

5. I think I'll be happy in our new house.   long e   long i

6. The house is large and sunny.   long e   long i

7. I hope I won't cry when I leave Kansas.   long e   long i

8. I will miss the beautiful sky!   long e   long i

Home-School Connection Think of two words with the letter **y**, each with the long **e** and long **i** sounds. Show your words to a family member.

Comprehension: A House of Grass

Use with Student Book pages 278–283.

Answer the questions about the reading.

Recall

1. Where does Molly reside?

_____

2. What kind of houses has Sarah seen on the prairie?

_____

3. What does Sarah's mom say is as thick as a mat?

_____

Comprehend

4. Compare and contrast Sarah and Molly's homes.

_____

_____

Analyze

5. How do you think you would adapt to living in a sod house on the prairie?

_____

_____

_____

Name _____ Date _____

Reader's Companion

Use with Student Book pages 278–283.

A House of Grass

Dear Molly,

I have funny news! We live in a sod house! It is dark and damp, but do not worry. It will protect us from the climate. It is an excellent shelter!

There are few trees on the prairie. The land looks like a sea of grass.

Love,

Sarah

Dear Sarah,

I would love to live near you again, but I would not like to live on the frontier! I prefer my life in Boston.

When I look out my window, I see churches, museums, and stores. These are strong buildings that were built to last forever. But even rain could hurt your buildings. Your house could turn to mud.

A sod house does not appeal to me. I certainly do not like grass or dirt. I do not want to live with bugs!

Love,

Molly

Use What You Know

List three things you know about sod houses.

1. _____

2. _____

3. _____

Reading Strategy

Underline one sentence that tells you why Sarah is writing to Molly.

Comprehension Check

Circle two sentences that tell you why Molly does not want to live on the prairie.

Use the Strategy

Why does Molly write to Sarah?

_____

_____

_____

Retell It!

Retell this passage as if you are Sarah writing to a friend. Describe your new life.

_____

_____

_____

_____

Reader's Response

Would you like to live in a sod house? Why or why not?

_____

_____

_____

Summarize the passage for a family member.

Name _____   Date _____

Learning Strategies: Author's Purpose

Use with Student Book pages 284–285.

Read each sentence to find out if the author's purpose is to entertain, persuade, or inform. The first one is done for you.

1. The winters on the prairie are harsh.

inform

2. You must read this wonderful book.

_____

3. The bugs in sod houses are delicious to eat.

_____

4. The sod on the prairie is very thick.

_____

5. Sod houses look a lot like today's houses.

_____

6. You will love my new home, so please visit.

_____

Home-School Connection   Write one sentence that compares a sod house to your home. Then write one sentence that contrasts a sod house with your home. Show your sentences to a family member.

Grammar: Prepositions and Prepositional Phrases

Use with Student Book pages 286–287.

Review the forms of **prepositions** and **prepositional phrases**.

> She is singing the song **for me**.
>
> The keys are **on the table**.
>
> The boy is running **around the corner**.

A. Complete each sentence using one of the prepositions.

for	by	until

Example: The climate <u>in</u> the summer is much nicer.

1. Did you build that house _____ the river?

2. I sat near my best friend _____ the teacher moved me.

3. During the game we cheered _____ our favorite team.

B. Underline *all* the prepositional phrases in each sentence. Then circle the word that each prepositional phrase describes.

Example: The (chair) <u>by the fire</u> is warm.

4. The class of fifth-graders is performing a play.

5. He rode his bike on the sidewalk.

6. She looked under the rock for worms.

Write five new sentences using the same prepositions used in Exercise A: *for, by,* and *until*. Share your sentences with a family member.

Name _____   Date _____

Spelling: Adding *-er* or *-r* to mean "more"

Use with Student Book pages 288–289.

Read each sentence. Write the word that means the same thing as the words in parentheses. The first one is done for you.

> **SPELLING TIP**
>
> Add *-er* to a word to mean "more." When a word ends in silent e, you only need to add *-r*.

1. Winters were _____ on

             (more harsh)

the prairie.

2. Cats are _____ than lions.

       (more small)

3. The trip took _____ than we thought.

       (more long)

4. A brick house is _____ than a sod house.

       (more strong)

5. Last week, the weather was _____.

       (more nice)

6. I think the grass is _____ in Kansas.

       (more green)

7. This apple is _____ than that one.

       (more ripe)

8. Which animal do you think is _____?

       (more smart)

9. It's much _____ in the forest.

       (more cold)

Home-School Connection

Write a new sentence for each of the spelling words. Show your sentences to a family member.

Writing: Organize Ideas by Problem and Solution

Read the paragraphs. Then read each question and circle the correct answer.

(1) I wanted to turn an empty lot near our school into a small community park. (2) But the lot was filled trash, bottles, and boxes. (3) There was no dirt to plant flowers and grass. (4) There were no lights or benches, either. (5) Without help, I wasn't sure how to make my dream come true.

(6) My teacher, Ms. Han, told our school about the problem. (7) Students and teachers worked together to clear out the lot. (8) We planted flowers and grass. (9) People gave us money. (10) We used it to buy lights and benches. (11) By working together we turned an empty lot into a beautiful park.

1. Which sentence should be added?

   A People really hated the lot because it was ugly.

   B We added trash cans and soft drink machines.

   C We brought in truckloads of good dirt.

   D Ms. Han then moved away.

2. Where should the sentence you chose in question 1 be added?

   A Before sentence 7

   B After sentence 2

   C Before sentence 8

   D After sentence 10

3. What is the BEST way to revise sentences 9 and 10?

   A We used the people gave us money to buy lights and benches.

   B People gave us money that we decided to use to buy lights and benches.

   C People gave us money that we used to buy lights and benches.

   D No revision is needed.

Name _____ Date _____

Key Words

Use with Student Book pages 290–291.

pioneer
homestead
settler
orchard
chapel

A. Read each clue. Unscramble the letters to write the word that matches the clue.

1. a place where fruit trees grow

ohrracd _____

2. a small church

alhcpe _____

3. a farmhouse and land

oeastedhm _____

4. a person who is among the first to explore an area

inrepoe _____

5. a person who makes a home where few people have lived before.

etrtsle _____

B. Read each sentence. Write TRUE or FALSE.

6. Orchards grow all kinds of vegetables like cucumbers and string beans. _____

7. Pioneers like to investigate old discoveries to make sure everything has been found. _____

8. A family usually resides in a homestead and farms the land. _____

9. A settler buys old houses and fixes them. _____

10. Chapels are very small and built with simple materials like wood. _____

175

Academic Words

Use with Student Book page 292.

considerable
labor
undertake

A. Choose the word that best completes each sentence. Write the word.

1. Pioneers had _____ courage to move their families to new places.

2. If the students _____ the bake sale, everyone in the class needs to bring cookies to sell.

3. A lot of _____ is needed to complete this math project.

B. Circle the word that *best* completes the sentence.

4. The group said they were ready for all the physical (labor/undertake) needed for this job.

5. If I (undertake/labor) more chores, my dad will pay me an allowance.

6. Pets require a (considerable/labor) amount of care.

C. Answer the questions.

7. What subject in school takes **considerable** work from you?

_____

_____

8. When you are older what job would you like to **undertake**?

_____

_____

Pretend you live in a cabin in the woods. List three amenities you would like to have. Show your list to a family member.

Name _____ Date _____

Phonics: *R*-Controlled *ar, or, ore*

Use with Student Book page 293.

> **The letter *r* changes the vowel sound.**
>
> | am | ton | toe |
> |---|---|---|
> | arm | torn | tore |

Read each sentence. Underline the words with the letters *ar* that have the same vowel sound as in *art*. Draw a box around the words with the letters *or* or *ore* that have the same vowel sound as in *torn* and *tore*.

1. How far is it to the store?

2. We are growing corn in the garden.

3. Every March we go to the shore.

4. The story was hard to read.

5. The pencil is sharp and costs forty cents.

6. We gave Renata a gift and a card for her birthday.

7. Did you come by car or bus?

8. They went to the park in the morning.

9. I tore my shirt in the backyard.

10. The pitcher's arm was sore.

Write two more words that have the vowel sound *ar* as in *march* and two that have the *or/ore* sound as in *torn* and *tore*. Show your words to a family member.

177

Comprehension: A Young Pioneer in Kansas

Use with Student Book pages 294–297.

Answer the questions about the reading.

Recall

1. Why did families like the Colts travel to the Kansas Territory?

_____

2. What was the Colts' stopover before they arrived in Kansas City, Missouri?

_____

3. Why did Miriam have to cook outside at first?

_____

Comprehend

4. Why did the Colts have to use their traveling trunks as chairs?

_____

_____

Analyze

5. Why did the pioneers learn to use common objects for other purposes?

_____

_____

_____

Name _____ Date _____

Reader's Companion

Use with Student Book pages 294–297.

A Young Pioneer in Kansas

There was a small cabin on the property that the Colts hoped to settle. As soon as he could, Mr. Colt got to work to make it a comfortable home. He smoothed the dirt floor in the cabin and put in flat stones. He built shelves to hold the family's tin cups and dishes.

For their bedding, Miriam filled large, cotton bags with dried prairie grass. Round pieces of logs served as table tops. The trunks in which the Colts had brought their clothes were used as chairs. Bags of flour and cornmeal were stored in a corner. The whole family slept and ate in one room. It was too small for a cooking fire, so Miriam cooked outside.

Use What You Know

List three things you know about how the pioneers lived.

1. _____

2. _____

3. _____

Reading Strategy

MARK the TEXT

Circle one sentence that helps you visualize how small their cabin was.

Comprehension Check

MARK the TEXT

Underline a sentence that explains what Mr. Colt did to make the cabin comfortable.

Use the Strategy

Tell how the pieces of logs were used in the cabin.

_____

_____

_____

Retell It!

Retell this passage as if you are visiting the Colts' cabin. Tell a friend what it is like.

_____

_____

_____

_____

_____

Reader's Response

Would you like to live in a log cabin? Why or why not?

_____

_____

_____

Summarize the passage for a family member.

180

Name _____   Date _____

Learning Strategies: Visualize

Use with Student Book pages 298–299.

Read each paragraph. Write words that helped you to visualize each scene.

1. It was a windy day. Sand blew into my face. Up in the sky, a blue kite danced in the wind. Suddenly, my big umbrella flew into the water.

   _____

   _____

2. Something was wrong. First the washing machine moved back and forth. Then it began to shake. Suddenly, the top popped open. Water spilled onto the floor. "What a mess!" Kelly thought.

   _____

   _____

3. The windows were broken. The front door made a loud noise when it opened. The paint was falling off the walls. My grandparents had used the barn to keep chickens. But now we use it as a playhouse.

   _____

   _____

4. It snowed for two days. The town was buried under snow. Amos stayed inside. He walked over to the window. It was covered in ice.

   _____

   _____

Tell a family member a fairy tale. Use words that will help the family member visualize the subject.

181

Grammar: Present Perfect

Use with Student Book pages 300–301.

Review the forms of the **present perfect**.

> We **have eaten** dinner already.
> Linda **has finished** her homework.

Write the present perfect form of the verbs in parentheses. Then write a sentence using the past perfect.

Example: (be) <u>have been</u>

He <u>has been</u> to the dentist.

1. (go) _____

_____

2. (labor) _____

_____

3. (grow) _____

_____

4. (play) _____

_____

5. (undertake) _____

_____

6. (arrive) _____

_____

 Write five more sentences using five new verbs and the present perfect tense. Share your sentences with a family member.

Name _____ Date _____

Spelling: Syllables

Use with Student Book pages 302–303.

Spell each of the words below by dividing it into syllables. The first one is done for you.

1. protect _____ pro tect _____

2. structures _____

3. treehouse _____

4. generations _____

5. themselves _____

6. natural _____

7. challenge _____

8. dangerous _____

9. architecture _____

10. backyards _____

Use three of the words to write a paragraph about a house.

_____

_____

_____

Home-School Connection Choose any five words. Say them aloud to a family member. Write the words by dividing them into syllables.

Writing: Write to Compare and Contrast

Read the paragraph. Then read each question and circle the correct answer.

(1) Baseball and soccer are both fun sports to play, but they are very different. (2) In baseball, you catch a ball with a glove and hit it with a bat. (3) In soccer, you kick the ball with your feet. (4) You can use your head, too, but not your hands. (5) In baseball, players take turns batting and running to the bases. (6) Sometimes they wait a long time. (7) In soccer, players run all the time. (8) I have played soccer for two years, while my brother has played baseball. (9) I like soccer better because there is more activity for every player.

1. What is the BEST way to revise sentence 3?
   A Add *the popular European game after soccer*
   B Change *you kick to you only kick*
   C Delete *with your feet*
   D No revision is needed.

2. Which sentence does NOT belong in this story?
   A Sentence 3
   B Sentence 6
   C Sentence 7
   D Sentence 8

3. Which sentence would add good information to this story?
   A They only get to run if they hit the ball.
   B Because you sit and wait, baseball can be boring.
   C A soccer ball is much larger than a baseball.
   D That way they get a lot more exercise.

4. Where should the sentence you chose in question 3 be put?
   A After sentence 1
   B Before sentence 7
   C After sentence 5
   D Before sentence 8

Name _____ Date _____

Review

Use with Student Book pages 254–303.

Answer the questions after reading Unit 5. You can go back and reread to help find the answers.

1. Which question is NOT answered by the end of *The Underground City?* Circle the letter of the correct answer.

  A How many people live in Coober Pedy?

  B Are the underground houses warm in the winter?

  C Why do people want to live in caves?

  D Are opals native to Coober Pedy?

2. Read the sentences. Circle the two homophones.

> It would be nice to visit Coober Pedy. Many of the houses are unusual. They are not made of wood or brick. They are in caves underground.

3. Read the sentence. Write **F** for fact or **O** for opinion.

Many people in Coober Pedy live in caves. _____

4. Which sentence needs a comma? Circle the letter of the correct answer.

  A Have you been to Coober Pedy?

  B It is a small town in Australia.

  C It reminded me of Tucson, Arizona.

  D My grandfather first visited the town on January 26 1965.

5. Circle the word that has the *y* with the long /i/ sound.

yellow   story   sorry   try

Read this passage from *A House of Grass*. Then answer questions 6 and 7.

> Dear Molly,
>
> I have funny news! We live in a sod house! It is dark and damp. But do not worry. It will protect us from the climate. It is an excellent shelter!
>
> Love,
> Sarah

6. Identify the genre of the passage.

    A friendly letter   **B** informational text   **C** how-to poster

7. Does Sarah like her new home on the prairie? How do you know?

_____

_____

8. Which sentence helps you to visualize a log cabin? Circle the letter of the correct answer.

    A Although the days were filled with work, the Colt family also had time for fun.
    B He smoothed the dirt floor in the cabin and put in flat stones.
    C The ability to grow plenty of food was important to pioneer families.
    D The children already knew to stay away from skunks!

9. Rewrite sentence D using the present perfect.

_____

Tell a family member something new you learned from this unit.

Copyright © by Pearson Education, Inc.

Name _____   Date _____

Writing Workshop: Write a Magazine or Newspaper Article

Read the passage. Then read each question on the next page and circle the correct answer.

Cougars Band Wins Awards

(1) The middle school band one an award in the all-state band competition last weekend in Concord. (2) The band received a second-place award from the Massachusetts Music Educators Association.

(3) The all-state band is a competition it included more than 70 school bands. (4) Each band played three pieces of music. (5) The judges were all band directors from universities across Massachusetts.

(6) As a result of their award, the band will travel to boston in February. (7) They will play in a special concert at the Massachusetts Music Educators Association Convention at the Boston Convention Center. (8) Congratulations to the Cougars band!

1. What change, if any, should be made in sentence 1?
   A Change *award* to *awards*
   B Change *weekend* to *week end*
   C Change *one* to *won*
   D Make no change

2. Which sentence could BEST be added after sentence 2?
   A Concord is far from our city.
   B This is the highest award our band has ever won.
   C They had to take the school bus to go there.
   D Band class is during the final period at our school.

3. What is the BEST way to revise sentence 3?
   A The all-state band competed more than 70 school bands.
   B The all-state band is a competition that more than 70 school bands.
   C The all-state band competition included more than 70 school bands.
   D No revision is needed.

4. What change, if any, should be made in sentence 4?
   A Change *pieces* to *piece*
   B Change *music* to *musics*
   C Change *pieces* to *of pieces*
   D Make no change

5. What change, if any, should be made in sentence 6?
   A Change *will travel* to *travel*
   B Change *result* to *results*
   C Change *boston* to *Boston*
   D Make no change

Name _____ Date _____

Fluency

Use with Student Book page 311.

How fast are you? Use a clock. Read the text about *A House of Grass*. How long did it take you? Write your time in the chart. Read three times.

A House of Grass tells of two young cousins who wrote letters to	13
each other long ago. In her letters, Sarah describes her new life in	26
Kansas, far away from cousin Molly who lives in Boston.	36
Sarah and her family travel by wagon to the Kansas prairie, where	48
she sees miles of grass and funny houses. The houses are not made	61
of wood or stone or bricks. They are made of thick prairie grass and	75
dirt. Sarah's new house is made of this sod. She tells Molly that	88
the house is dark and damp, but that the thick walls of her house	102
protect her from the climate, and keep her warm in winter and	114
cool in summer. Molly tells Sarah she doesn't want to live with	126
dirt and bugs!	129

My Times

Learning Checklist

Word Study and Phonics

☐ Homophones

☐ *Y* as a Vowel

☐ R-Controlled: *ar, or, ore*

Strategies

☐ Fact and Opinion

☐ Author's Purpose

☐ Visualize

Grammar

☐ Capitalizing Proper Nouns

☐ Prepositions and Prepositional Phrases

☐ Present Perfect

Writing

☐ Write to Classify

☐ Organize by Problem and Solution

☐ Write to Compare and Contrast

☐ Writing Workshop: Write a Magazine or Newspaper Article

Listening and Speaking

☐ Present a TV Talk Show

Name _____ Date _____

Test Preparation

Use with Student Book pages 312–313.

Read the selection. Then answer the questions.

Prairie Dogs

1 A prairie dog is a rodent that is about the size of a rabbit. Prairie dogs are very social animals. Many species live together underground in large networks of burrows called towns. The towns can cover one half of a square mile and house hundreds of animals. The towns have special rooms where prairie dogs store food and raise their young.

2 Prairie dogs may share their burrows with other animals such as snakes, burrowing owls, and ferrets. They feed on grass during the day. They guard the entrances to their towns. If a predator comes, the guard prairie dog barks to warn others.

1. Where are many prairie dogs most likely to live?
   A In underground burrows
   B On hill tops
   C With rabbits
   D In Arctic towns

2. In paragraph 1, <u>social</u> means _____.
   F liking to be with others
   G living in tiny burrows
   H a friendly gathering
   J predatory

3. What is one way in which prairie dogs protect one another?
   A They store food and raise their young.
   B They gather grass for all of them to eat.
   C They share their homes with rabbits.
   D They guard the entrances to their towns.

4. Which sentence from the story tells what prairie dogs eat?
   F They feed on grass during the day.
   G Prairie dogs are very social animals.
   H Prairie dogs may share their burrows with other animals such as snakes, burrowing owls, and ferrets.
   J If a predator comes, the guard prairie dog barks to warn others.

Read the selection. Then answer the questions.

Bats

1 Bats are amazing animals. Scientists say there are over 1,000 different kinds of bats in the world. They can be found on all continents of the world except Antarctica. Many movies show bats as scary animals, but most bats are very helpful. Most bats eat insects and fruit. They help control the insect population.

2 Bats like to eat at night. Many bats use *echolocation* to move around. In echolocation, bats send out tiny sounds. People cannot hear these sounds. The sounds bounce off objects, and bats can hear them. Bats use echolocation to find their way around, and to look for food at night.

1. In paragraph 1, *population* means _____.
   A Kinds of insects
   B Number of insects
   C Flight of insects
   D Control of insects

2. In paragraph 1, control means _____.
   F Expand
   G Limit
   H Feed
   J Spray

3. On how many continents can bats NOT be found?
   A 3
   B 2
   C 4
   D 1

4. Bats use their _____ to find their way around at night.
   F Eyes
   G Ears
   H Wings
   J Mouths

Name _____ Date _____

Key Words

Use with Student Book pages 320–321.

signatures
mission
astronaut
plaque
explorer
surrounded

B. **Choose the word that *best* completes each sentence. Write the word.**

7. The crew's _____ was to reach the moon.

8. A safe campfire is _____ by stones.

9. Each winner's name is on the _____ .

10. My friends put their _____ on my birthday card.

11. Ernest Shackleton was the first _____ to reach the South Pole.

12. An _____ named Neil Armstrong walked on the moon.

A. **Match each word with its definition. Write the letter of the correct answer.**

1. astronaut _____ **A** to be all around something

2. surrounded _____ **B** person who travels to an unknown place

3. signatures _____ **C** person who flies into space

4. plaque _____ **D** metal or stone with writing on it

5. explorer _____ **E** a group's goal or plan

6. mission _____ **F** names written on a piece of paper

Academic Words

Use with Student Book page 322.

achieve
community
unique

A. Choose the word that *best* completes each sentence. Write the word.

1. All the people in the _____ helped clean up the streets after the big storm.

2. Every person has their own _____ set of fingerprints.

3. The boys practiced hard every day to _____ their goals.

B. Choose the word that best matches the meaning of the underlined words. Write the word.

4. She has a very <u>special</u> singing voice. _____

5. The most important thing to her right now is to <u>have success</u> in school. _____

6. The committee tried to take care of the needs of the <u>neighborhood</u>.

_____

C. Answer the questions.

7. What are some things you like about your **community**?

_____

8. What is something you hope to **achieve** on your own?

_____

9. What kind of **unique** talents would you like to have?

_____

 **Draw pictures to illustrate two vocabulary words. Label each picture with the word. Show your pictures to a family member.**

Name _____ Date _____

Phonics: Diphthongs: *ow* and *ou*

Use with Student Book page 323.

> The letters *ow* and *ou* can have the vowel sound you hear in *how* and *loud*.
>
> The letters *ow* can also have the long *o* sound you hear in *low*.

A. Read each sentence. Underline the words with *ow* that have the long *o* sound as in *low*. Draw a box around the words with *ow* or *ou* that have the vowel sound as in *plow* and *loud*.

1. Flowers need water to grow.

2. The brown cow walked slowly across the field.

3. Show me your new house.

4. What sound does an owl make?

B. Write each word in the correct column.

below	blow	cloud	down	glow	town

ow as in *low*	*ow* as in *plow*; *ou* as in *round*

Home-School Connection Write two words for each of the spelling/sound patterns. Show your words to a family member.

Comprehension: The Moon Tree

Use with Student Book pages 324–331.

Answer the questions about the reading.

Recall

1. What was on the stone that rested against a tall sycamore tree?

_____

2. What did Hector and Stuart read about at the library?

_____

3. What did the boys ask people to do?

_____

Comprehend

4. What did Hector and Stuart learn about moon trees?

_____

_____

Analyze

5. How did Mrs. Wu help the boys achieve their goal?

_____

_____

_____

Name _____ Date _____

Reader's Companion

Use with Student Book pages 324–331.

The Moon Tree

They called themselves the Moon Tree Crew. Then Stuart named the tree. He said, "Our moon tree needs a name. People will care more about a tree called . . . Apollo."

Stuart knew about these things. His father worked in the advertising business.

Mrs. Wu made posters. Each poster had a slogan: "Save Apollo, the moon tree."

The boys and their friends were busy. Some went to stores, others walked down Main Street. They told people the moon tree's story. The whole town wanted to help. The Moon Tree Crew got hundreds of signatures.

Use What You Know

List three things you would like to save.

1. _____

2. _____

3. _____

Comprehension Check

The special tree is going to be cut down. Draw a line through one sentence that tells what the boys do to solve this problem.

Learning Strategy

Underline one place where the characters are talking about a solution.

Use the Strategy

Mrs. Wu and the boys had a problem. They wanted to get people to care about the moon tree. What was their solution?

_____

_____

_____

Retell It!

Retell the passage. as if you are Stuart or Hector and you just found the moon tree.

_____

_____

_____

_____

Reader's Response

How else could Hector and Stuart have saved the tree?

_____

_____

_____

Retell the passage to a family member.

Name _____ Date _____

Learning Strategies: Problem and Solution

Use with Student Book pages 332–333.

Read the passage. Then fill in the Problem and Solution Chart.

Our Park

My friends and I often took the bus to the park. But it was far away. One day, I had an idea. "Let's make our own park. We can use the vacant lot."

"It's filled with trash," said Jessie.

"There are no trees," said Yolanda.

I smiled. "We have lots of work to do!"

We cleaned the lot. We threw away the garbage.

"Something is missing," said Jessie.

"It's not very pretty," said Yolanda.

They were right. We needed some plants. The next day, Mom bought flowers and bushes. Finally, the lot looked like a park.

"All we need now is a place to sit," I said to Mom.

The next day, Dad bought a picnic table and chairs.

"Our park is nicer than a vacant lot," we said.

Problem	Solution
	The kids take the bus to the park.
The vacant lot is dirty.	
	The kids plant flowers and bushes in the park.
There is no place to sit.	

Write a paragraph about a problem you had and how you solved the problem. Show your paragraph to a family member.

Grammar: Compound Sentences: *and, but, or*

Use with Student Book pages 334–335.

Review **compound sentences** using *and, but,* and *or* below.

> The boys went to the park, and they played a game of baseball.
> The boys wanted to play baseball, but it was raining.
> The could play baseball, or they could play a game of soccer.

Use the connecting words *and, but,* or *or* to combine the sentences. Write the new sentence.

Example: Mary went shopping. She bought a new dress.
<u>Mary went shopping, and she bought a new dress.</u>

1. Jake wants to be a doctor. He doesn't like to study.

_____

2. The man walked into the store. He asked for turkey sandwich.

_____

3. She wants to take a trip to New York. She wants to take a trip to Chicago.

_____

4. My mother works during the day. She takes care of us at night.

_____

5. He could be a good musician. He doesn't practice enough.

_____

 **Home-School Connection** Write five sentences about your day using *and, but,* or *or*. Share your ideas with a family member.

Name _____   Date _____

Spelling: Silent *gh*

Use with Student Book pages 336–337.

Read each clue. Spell a word with silent *gh* to solve each clue.

SPELLING TIP

The letters *gh* are sometimes silent. Notice words with silent *gh* and learn their spellings.

1. opposite of *low*

_____

2. another word for *correct* _____

3. number between seven and nine _____

4. opposite of *dark* _____

5. very shiny _____

6. how tall you are _____

7. opposite of *day* _____

8. how heavy you are _____

 Write a paragraph about yourself. Use three of the answer words.

_____

_____

_____

_____

_____

 Write four more words with the silent *gh*. Show your words to a family member.

Writing: Plan a Research Report

Fill in the charts to prepare for your own research report.

Choose a topic. Write questions and answers about the topic.

Broad Topic	
Question:	
Answer:	

Write more questions to narrow down the topic. Which one do you want as your research question?

1. _____

2. _____

3. _____

Make a research plan.

What do I want to know?	Where can I find it?

Name _____ Date _____

Key Words

Use with Student Book pages 338–339.

thrive
hiking
trails
thrilling
canyon
ledge

A. Read each clue. Underline the key word in the row of letters. Then write the word.

1. to grow quickly or be in good health   dlelthrivekdge   _____

2. taking a long walk through the woods   triehikingonh   _____

3. full of excitement   sluiwthrillingc   _____

4. land at the bottom of hills   rtcanyonpibs   _____

5. paths or walkways   dilztrailsjafve   _____

B. Write TRUE or FALSE.

6. Amusement park rides can be thrilling. _____

7. A canyon is at the top of a hill. _____

8. Standing on a ledge can be dangerous. _____

9. Plants thrive when it rains often. _____

10. Hiking trails are found in trees. _____

Academic Words

Use with Student Book page 340.

A. Match each word with its definition. Write the letter of the correct answer.

1. equipped _____   **A** to be excited to do something

2. route _____   **B** to have what you need

3. motivated _____   **C** the way from one place to another

B. Choose the word that *best* completes each sentence. Write the word.

> equipped
> motivated
> route

4. A straight line is the fastest _____ to any destination.

5. If you plan to build something, you need to be _____ with the correct tools first.

6. The young man was very _____ to win the race.

C. Answer the questions.

7. Why is it a good idea to plan your **route** before you go someplace?

_____

8. What are you **motivated** to do right now?

_____

9. What is an activity that people should be correctly **equipped** for?

_____

Use the vocabulary words to tell a story about a unicorn that lives on the side of a mountain. Tell your story to a family member.

Name _____ Date _____

Phonics: Variant Vowel *oo*

Use with Student Book page 341.

> Sometimes the letters *oo* have the sound you hear in *hook*.
> Sometimes the letters *oo* have the sound you hear in *soon*.

A. Read each sentence. Underline the words with *oo* that have the sound you hear in *took*. Draw a box around the words with *oo* that have the sound you hear in *soon*.

1. Did you have a good time at school today?

2. My wool coat has a hood.

3. The goose ran into the woods.

4. Look at the bright moon!

5. Noodles are my favorite food.

6. Yesterday afternoon we baked cookies.

B. Write each word in the correct column.

> book   cool   hook   room

oo as in *too*	*oo* as in *hook*

Home-School Connection Add two words to each column of the chart. Show the chart to a family member.

205

Comprehension: A Hike Back in Time

Use with Student Book pages 342–349.

Answer the questions about the reading.

Recall

1. Why did the narrator want to go to the Grand Canyon?

_____

2. Who did the family meet in Supai?

_____

3. Where did the family hike to?

_____

Comprehend

4. What did the narrator wonder about on her first day at the Grand Canyon?

_____

_____

Analyze

5. How is the narrator like her grandmother?

_____

_____

_____

Name _____ Date _____

Reader's Companion

Use with Student Book pages 342–349.

A Hike Back in Time

We heard the faint sound of water in the distance. As we walked, the noise got louder. The air felt cooler. Then we turned a corner, and the trail stopped. I saw a tall waterfall pouring into a clear pool.

"Mooney Falls!" I cried.

I glanced at my grandmother's picture. "It looks just like it did fifty years ago."

I dipped my hand into the cool water and let it pour through my fingers. I wondered if my grandmother had done the same thing.

"We should go back," Dad said. "But first, we need a picture."

I stood in front of the waterfall while Dad pulled the camera out of his bag.

"Wait a second," Mom said. She picked up a stick from the side of the trail. "You need a walking stick. Now, you look just like your grandmother."

I looked at the picture again and then held it up. "Grandmother and I are visiting the waterfall together!"

Use What You Know

List three things you know about waterfalls.

1. _____

2. _____

3. _____

Comprehension Check

Why did the main character take a picture at the falls?

Reading Strategy

Circle two sentences that tell you something about the setting.

Use the Strategy

The girl says, "Grandmother and I are visiting the waterfall together!"
What does she mean?

_____

_____

_____

Retell It!

Retell this passage. List in order three of the things the family heard
and saw.

_____

_____

_____

_____

Reader's Response

What older friend or family member is special to you? Why?

_____

_____

_____

Retell the passage to a family member.

Name _____ Date _____

Learning Strategies: Plot and Setting

Use with Student Book pages 350–351.

Read the passage. Then fill in the chart.

My Name Is Filbert

The Chang family walked along the beach in Cape Cod. The beaches of Cape Cod are beautiful. Shells and colored rocks glow in the sun. Usually, the Changs saw birds and crabs on their walks. But one day, they saw a puppy sitting in the sand.

"I think it's lost," said Mrs. Chang.

Jimmy pointed to the dog's neck. "Look," he said. "It has a dog tag." Mr. Chang read the dog tag. "My name is Filbert." There was a phone number on the tag.

Mrs. Chang reached into her pocket. She pulled out her phone. Soon, two small children and their father came running towards the beach. "Filbert!" they shouted. "Where have you been?"

Filbert ran toward them.

"Thank you!" said the man. "We were very worried about our new puppy!"

Setting	**1.** Where are the Changs? _____
	2. What is it like there? _____
Plot	**3.** What happens first? _____
	4. What happens next? _____
	5. What happens at the end? _____

Imagine the story continued. Tell a family member two more things that could happen.

Grammar: Past Progressive

Use with Student Book pages 352–353.

Review the rules for forming the **past progressive** below.

was, were + infinitive + *-ing*	I *was studying* until 10 o'clock last night.
was, were + *not* + infinitive + *-ing*	I *was not studying* until 10 o'clock last night.

Complete each sentence with the past progressive tense of the verb in parentheses.

Example: (plan) They <u>were planning</u> to visit the museum this week.

1. (play) The kids _____ while their parents made dinner.

2. (not eat) She _____ a bar of chocolate.

3. (run) The dog _____ around in circles.

4. (practice) That's the same music we _____ last week.

5. (study) The boys _____ hard for the exam all last week.

6. (not play) The woman _____ the piano.

7. (visit) We _____ my parents when she called.

8. (ride) Bart _____ his bicycle when it started to rain.

9. (happen) What _____ during the start of the game?

10. (hike) My brother _____ in Yosemite last month.

 **Write five sentences using the past progressive. Share your ideas with a family member.**

Name _____ Date _____

Spelling: Homophones

Use with Student Book pages 354–355.

Read the sentences that follow *a* and *b*. Then write the homophone that completes the sentences. The first one is done for you.

SPELLING TIP

Learn common homophones. Make sure you use the correct homophone in your writing. Check a dictionary to be sure.

1. A Do you know the

_____ way _____ to school?

I'm lost!

B Your puppy is getting really big! How much does he

_____ weigh _____?

2. A I did well on the test. All of my answers were

_____ !

B Did you _____ your name at the top of
the page?

3. A It's such a hot day! The _____ is so bright!

B My _____ is five years old. He calls
me Daddy.

4. A What do you want to _____ when you
grow up?

B Have you ever been stung by a _____ ?

Look up the dictionary definitions for *peace/piece* and *great/grate*. Then use each word in a sentence. Share your sentences with a family member.

211

Writing: Paraphrasing a Source

Fill in the charts with information to prepare for your own research report.

Choose two paragraphs from one or more of your sources. Express the ideas in your own words. Then list the citation for each paraphrase.

Text from Source	Paraphrase	Citation

Text from Source	Paraphrase	Citation

Name _____ Date _____

Key Words

Use with Student Book pages 356–357.

worth
trade
bartered
currency
rulers

A. Choose the word that *best* completes each sentence. Write the word.

1. Many young people who collect baseball cards _____ cards with other collectors.

2. Travelers to foreign countries often have to change their money to the _____ used by that country.

3. An item that is produced in limited quantities is usually _____ more than an item that is mass produced.

4. Early American settlers often _____ with neighboring settlements to get the things they needed to live.

5. A country's money often shows an image of the country's _____ throughout history.

B. Read each sentence. Circle the word that correctly completes the sentence.

6. On our trip abroad, we changed our American dollars for the (worth/currency) of each country we visited.

7. After he bought the car, he found out that it was (bartered/worth) less than what he had paid.

8. Sports teams often (currency/trade) players with one another.

9. A country's (rulers/trade) often influence the way they get along with other countries.

10. Early settlers (worth/bartered) with Native Americans in order to get what they did not have.

Academic Words

Use with Student Book page 358.

> cooperate
> initial
> tradition

A. Choose the word that *best* completes each sentence. Write the word.

1. Those girls always _____ so well with each other.

2. Their family has a _____ of going out for dinner together every Friday night.

3. The girl's _____ reaction to the big dog was fear, but then she realized he was friendly.

B. Choose the word that best matches the meaning of the underlined words. Write the word.

4. It is important for a team to <u>work well together</u>. _____

5. The <u>first</u> reaction he had was to run. _____

6. He has a <u>practice</u> of sitting quietly by himself for ten minutes every day.

_____

C. Answer the questions.

7. Does your family have any unique **traditions**? What are they?

_____

8. What is something that you had a bad **initial** reaction to?

_____

Home-School Connection Ask a family member to share his or her favorite school memory. Then tell your favorite school memory. List two ways your school memories are different and two ways they are similar.

Name _____ Date _____

Word Study: Greek and Latin Roots

Use with Student Book page 359.

> **Many English words come from Greek or Latin roots.**

Read each sentence. Write the Greek or Latin root that each underlined word comes from. The first one is done for you.

Latin Roots	Greek Roots
flex: bend	*geo*: earth
vac: to empty	*gram*: letter
rupt: break	*scope*: to see
mar: sea	*ast*: star

1. An <u>astronaut</u> travels into space. ast _____

2. A volcano can have a violent <u>eruption</u>. _____

3. He is an athlete so he has good <u>reflexes</u>. _____

4. I like to learn all about different countries in the world. I love to study <u>geography</u>. _____

5. The <u>submarine</u> travels deep in the ocean. _____

6. You can see the moon with a <u>telescope</u>. _____

7. They used to send to <u>telegrams</u> instead of calling on the phone.

_____

8. I <u>vacuum</u> the rug every Saturday so that it is clean. _____

 **Write as many words using Greek and Latin roots as you can. Show your words to a family member.**

Comprehension: The History of Money

Use with Student Book pages 360–361.

Answer the questions about the reading.

Recall

1. What was the first "money"?

_____

2. Who began using metals to make shells about 3,000 years ago?

_____

3. When did people in Europe begin using paper money?

_____

Comprehend

4. How are computers changing the way we use money?

_____

_____

Analyze

5. Why would metal be a better material than shells for early currency?

_____

_____

_____

Name _____ Date _____

Reader's Companion

Use with Student Book pages 360–361.

The History of Money

The first "money" was animals. Then, when people began to farm, they traded vegetables, fruits, and grains. But people wanted money that was easier to carry. That's why early cultures around the world used shells as currency. People agreed on the value of each shell. Then they used shells to buy or sell things. In North America, Native Americans and Europeans used shells until the 1800s.

About 3,000 years ago, people in China began using metals to make shells. Then they made coins. Slowly, metal currency spread to other countries. People made coins from gold, silver, or bronze. The coins were stamped with art or images, such as rulers' faces.

Use What You Know

List three things you know about early currency.

1. _____

2. _____

3. _____

Comprehension Check

How long did Native Americans and Europeans use shells as currency? Underline the text that tells you this.

Learning Strategy

Why did people want to stop using animals as currency? Circle the text that tells you this.

Use the Strategy

Describe how the use of shells as currency began.

_____

_____

_____

Retell It!

Retell the passage as if you are an early traveler who uses different types of currency.

_____

_____

_____

_____

Reader's Response

Do you think in the future people will only use computers to buy and sell things rather than actual currency? Why or why not?

_____

_____

_____

Copyright © by Pearson Education, Inc.

Tell a family member about the history of money.

Name _____ Date _____

Learning Strategies: Summarize

Use with Student Book pages 364–365.

Read the poem. Then answer the questions.

The Pioneers

Across the plains
And over the hills
They traveled
Long ago

In search of land
And open fields
In places
They did not know.

From east to west
On horses and wagons
With dreams
And great hopes, too

The story of
The pioneers
Pleases
Both me and you.

1. Who is the poem about?

_____

2. What did they do?

_____

3. Where did they go?

_____

4. When did they do it?

_____

5. Why did they go?

_____

Think of a poem you have read. Summarize that poem for a family member.

219

Grammar: Complex Sentences: *because, so*

Use with Student Book pages 366–367.

Review the forms of complex sentences using *because* and *so* below.

> He was late for work **because** he got a flat tire.
> He was tired **so** he took a short nap.
> **Because** he got a flat tire, he was late for work.
> **So** he could get some rest, he took a nap.

Complete these complex sentences using *because* or *so*.

Example: They were <u>happy</u> because the show as a big success.

1. John wants to lose weight _____ he goes to the gym every day.

2. _____ it rained, the concert was canceled.

3. She was not feeling well _____ she went to the hospital.

4. _____ they could see better, they moved to the front of the class.

5. The organizers scheduled the meeting in the afternoon _____ that all of the members could come.

6. _____ the community was so friendly, they always welcomed new people.

7. It was a hot, summer day _____ they decided to have some ice cream.

8. Karen didn't ride the Ferris wheel _____ she is afraid of heights.

 **Write five complex sentences using *because* and *so*. Share your ideas with a family member.**

Name _____   Date _____

Spelling: The /j/ Sound
Use with Student Book pages 368–369.

A. Read each clue. Write the word that matches the clue.

bridge	cages	garage
huge	orange	page

1. you turn it in a book

_____

2. zoo animals live in these

_____

3. this word names a color and a fruit _____

4. another word for *big* _____

5. a car drives over it to cross a river _____

6. place where you park a car _____

B. Write about a place you visited. Use at least two answer words.

_____

_____

_____

_____

Copyright © by Pearson Education, Inc.

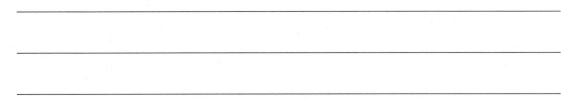

SPELLING TIP

At the end of a word, the sound /j/ can be spelled *-ge* or *-dge*.
• If a long vowel comes before /j/, use *-ge*.
• If a consonant comes before /j/, use *-ge*.
• If a short vowel comes before /j/, use *-dge*.

Home-School Connection Think of four more words with the /j/ sound spelled *-ge* and *-dge*. Write a sentence using each word. Tell a family member your sentences.

Writing: Quoting a Source

Fill in the charts with information to prepare for your own research report.

Choose two quotations you would like to use in your report. Fill in the charts. List the citation for the quotations.

Information Search	Direct Quote	Citation

Information Search	Direct Quote	Citation

Name _____   Date _____

Review

Use with Student Book pages 314–369.

Answer the questions after reading Unit 6. You can go back and reread to help find the answers.

1. Which question is not answered by the end of *The Moon Tree*? Circle the letter of the correct answer.

    A Who are the Moon Tree Crew?

    B How does Mrs. Wu help Hector and Stuart?

    C Does Mr. Bowman spare the tree?

    D Why do people sign the petition?

2. Read these sentences from the story.

> Hector held up a paper. "This is a petition," he said. "It says, 'The moon tree is an important part of history. It is too valuable to lose. Please spare our moon tree.' We need everybody in town to sign this petition."

What does *petition* mean?

    A signature   **C** written request

    B save   **D** valuable

3. Mr. Bowman wants to build a shopping mall. Why is that a problem for Hector and Stuart?

_____

4. Which underlined word does NOT have the *o* sound you hear in *loud*? Circle the letter of the correct answer.

    A Hector <u>found</u> the ball next to a strange, flat stone.

    B Hector ran to get Stuart <u>without</u> noticing the red flags.

    C Hector and Stuart knew <u>how</u> to save the moon tree.

    D Mrs. Wu said that the <u>woods</u> would be gone soon.

5. Read this sentence from *A Hike Back in Time*. Rewrite the sentence adding the correct quotation marks and punctuation.

I wonder if that's the trail to the waterfall I said to my parents.

_____

6. Read these sentences from *A Hike Back in Time*. Circle the word with the letters *oo* that has the sound you hear in *took*.

I dipped my hand into the cool water and let it pour through my fingers.
I stood in front of the waterfall while Dad pulled the camera out of his bag.

7. Circle the sentence that does NOT belong in a summary of *The History of Money*.

A My parents buy everything we need online.
B People weighed coins to learn their value.
C The first "money" was animals.
D Early cultures used shells as currency.

8. There is a compound word in one of the answers to Question 7. Write the compound word.

_____

9. When did people in Europe first use paper money?

A about 1650
B historians are not sure
C 1776
D after the Americans did

Tell a family member something new you learned from this unit.

Name _____ Date _____

Writing Workshop: Write a Research Report

Read the passage. Then read each question on the next page and circle the correct answer.

Statehood Day

(1) Statehood Day is a special day in Kentucky and Tennessee. (2) It is celebrated every year on June 1.

(3) Statehood Day celebrates Kentucky and Tennessee becoming the 15th and 16th states of the United States. (4) Kentucky became the 15th state on june 1, 1792. (5) Tennessee became the 16th state on June 1, 1796.

(6) Statehood Day reminds people of the importance of civic involvement. (7) People re-enact historical events, cook colonial food, and display arts and craft. (8) They show what life was like in the 1790s. (9) Many people go there to have fun and learn about their history at the same time.

1. What change should be made in sentence 4?

   A Change *june* to *June*

   B Change *became* to *becomes*

   C Change *join* to *joined*

   D Change *on* to *in*

2. Which sentence could BEST be added before sentence 4?

   A I live in Kentucky and my aunt lives in Tennessee.

   B They joined the United States four years apart, but on the same day.

   C That was more than 200 years ago.

   D Many other states joined later.

3. What change, if any, should be made in sentence 6?

   A Change *Day* to *day*

   B Change *reminds* to *remembers*

   C Change *importance* to *important*

   D Make no change

4. What change, if any, should be made in sentence 7?

   A Change *events* to *event*

   B Change *cook* to *cooks*

   C Change *craft* to *crafts*

   D Make no change

5. What is the BEST way to revise sentence 9?

   A Many people has fun and learns about their history at the same time.

   B Many people have fun and learn about their history at the same time.

   C Many people has fun and learn about its history at the same time.

   D No revision is needed.

Name _____   Date _____

Fluency

Use with Student Book page 379.

How fast are you? Use a clock. Read the text about *The Moon Tree*. How long did it take you? Write your time in the chart. Read three times.

The Moon Tree tells the story of Hector, who found his ball in	13
the woods. He found a special tree there, too. He read a brass	26
plaque that said the tree came from seeds that went to the	38
moon with the Apollo 14 astronauts.	43
Hector told his friend Stuart and the librarian Mrs. Wu about	55
the tree. Mrs. Wu told Hector that the moon tree would be cut	68
down so that Mr. Bowman could build a new shopping mall	79
there. Hector wanted to save the tree, and so he made a plan	92
with Stuart and Mrs. Wu. They created a petition for people in	104
the community to sign. They took the petition to Mr. Bowman,	115
who saw all the names. The special moon tree was saved.	126

My Times

Learning Checklist

Word Study and Phonics

☐ Diphthongs: *ow* and *ou*

☐ Variant Vowel: *oo*

☐ Greek and Latin Roots

Strategies

☐ Problem and Solution

☐ Plot and Setting

☐ Summarize

Grammar

☐ Compound Sentences: *and, but, or*

☐ Past Progressive

☐ Complex Sentences: *because, so*

Writing

☐ Plan a Research Report

☐ Paraphrasing a Source

☐ Quoting a Source

☐ Writing Workshop: Write a Research Report

Listening and Speaking

☐ Give an Oral Report

Name _____ Date _____

Test Preparation

Use with Student Book pages 380–381.

Read the selection. Look for any corrections and improvements that may be needed, then answer the questions.

(1) The city where I live has three interesting museums. (2) They are the Museum of History the Museum of Archaeology, and the Museum of Art. (3) The Museum of History is the largest of the three. (4) I live close to the Museum of History I go there a lot. (5) My mom is a volunteer at some of the events. (6) She says "if you come to our city, try to visit this museum. (7) I agree. (8) There is something for everyone here.

1. What change, if any, should be made in sentence 1?
   - **A** Change *three* to 3
   - **B** Change *The city* to *The City*
   - **C** Change *has* to *have*
   - **D** Make no change

2. What change, if any, should be made in sentence 2?
   - **F** Delete the comma after **Archaeology**
   - **G** Insert a comma after **History**
   - **H** Change *They are* to **They were**
   - **J** Make no change

3. What change, if any, should be made in sentence 4?
   - **A** I go to the museum of History a lot.
   - **B** I go to the close by Museum of History.
   - **C** I live close to the Museum of History, so I go there a lot.
   - **D** No revision is needed.

4. What is the BEST way to revise sentence 6?
   - **F** She says, "if you come to El Paso." Try to visit this museum
   - **G** She says "If you come to El Paso try to visit this museum."
   - **H** She says if you come to El Paso, try to visit this museum."
   - **J** She says, "If you come to El Paso, try to visit this museum."

229

Read the selection. Look for any corrections and improvements that may be needed, then answer the questions.

(1) The Texas Folklife Festival takes place every summer in San Antonio, Texas. (2) The festival held the Institute of Texan Cultures, part of the University of Texas at San Antonio. (3) The festival brings together people from more than 40 different cultural groups in Texas. (4) They share their tradition at the three-day festival, such as the special food, music, dance, arts, and crafts of their cultures. (5) The money from the festival is given back to the different cultural groups, so that they can continue to pass their traditions on to the next generations of Texans.

1. What change, if any, should be made in sentence 1?
   A Delete the comma after **San Antonio**
   B Change *San Antonio* to **San antonio**
   C Change *takes* to **take**
   D Make no change

2. What is the BEST way to revise sentence 2?
   F The festival holds the Institute of Texan Cultures, part of the University of Texas at San Antonio.
   G The festival is held by the Institute of Texan Cultures, part of the University of Texas at San Antonio.
   H The festival is held by the Institute of Texan Cultures part of the University of Texas at San Antonio.
   J No revision is needed.

3. What change, if any, should be made in sentence 3?
   A Delete **together**
   B Insert a comma after **people**
   C Change *festivals* to **festival**
   D Make no change

4. What change, if any, should be made in sentence 4?
   F Change *tradition* to **traditions**
   G Delete comma after **arts**
   H Change *their tradition* to **there tradition**
   J No revision is needed.